ALSO BY EDWARD SABIN

A Wider Horizon: The Primavera Journals of Ray Sabin (Editor)

Searching
FOR LIFE'S PURPOSE
still working on it

BY

Edward Sabin

WITH Amy Woods Butler

STORY SCRIBE BOOKS
Kansas City   St. Louis

STORY SCRIBE BOOKS

Kansas City   St. Louis

A division of The Story Scribe
www.thestoryscribe.com
816-377-8694

Note from Ed Sabin: This book is a personal recollection of my life, written with as much clarity and truth as my subjective perspective allows.

Copyright © 2022 Edward Sabin

Cover and layout design by Janet Muhm

All rights reserved
Printed in the United States of America

ISBN: 978-1-7327689-6-3
E-book ISBN: 978-1-7327689-7-0

Library of Congress Control Number: 2022935580

To my sister Nancy,
who asked me to write my story and by some miracle kept old family letters and our father's journals,

and to my sister Mimi,
who encouraged and helped me remember people and places

TABLE OF CONTENTS

Chapter 1	Chicago	1
Chapter 2	From Big City to Small Town	9
Chapter 3	Peabody	21
Chapter 4	Journey to Paraguay	29
Chapter 5	The Bruderhof	37
Chapter 6	A New Start	47
Chapter 7	Evergreen	53
Chapter 8	Planting Roots	59
Chapter 9	Finishing High School	69
Chapter 10	Park College	81
Chapter 11	University of Colorado	89
Chapter 12	The Big Trip	95
Chapter 13	On the Move	105
Chapter 14	From Europe to Home	117
Chapter 15	Back to School	125
Chapter 16	Slogging Through	131
Chapter 17	Small Town Teaching	137
Chapter 18	Back to City Life	143
Chapter 19	With the Trimaran to Texas	149
Chapter 20	Late-Blooming Hippie	155
Chapter 21	Go West, Lost Man	159
Chapter 22	Joining the Establishment	167
Chapter 23	Love and Marriage	175

CHAPTER ONE

Chicago

It's been a wonderful trip. I wouldn't have missed it for the world. The first half of my eighty plus years had many high highs but also low lows. The second half of my life has been more conventional, more on an even keel. I enjoyed travel and adventure in my youth—probably more than most people—but the flip side was a prolonged adolescence trying to figure out who I was and what I wanted to do with my life.

Being a PK (preacher's kid) explains some of my searching, as does having moved around a great deal while growing up (such as attending three different ninth grades). I was fortunate to have been raised in a loving family and to have received a good education.

My earliest memories are a collection of sensory experiences: the loud BANG, BANG, BANG as the trolley conductor flipped the seat backs before his drive back south on Blackstone Street; the chiming of the bells from the tall tower of the University of Chicago's Rockefeller Chapel; summer nights on the rooftop listening to the radio as fans churned the air; the feel of the cold, smooth granite pedestal that supported a bronze frieze on the Midway.

My family moved several times in the early years. I don't remember the places we lived—all rentals, as home ownership and the means to acquire it lay decades in the future—but some left impressions on my older sisters. One was a West Side residence where the girls were quarantined, along with our mother, during a bout of scarlet fever. Another was an apartment building next door to a tombstone factory where uncut stones littered the yard, offering neighborhood kids countless hiding places.

My parents had met in Chicago where both had migrated, she for art classes and city life, he for a job. In some ways they were alike and in others very different.

Betty in Prescott, Arkansas

Betty Davis was a Southerner, an attractive young woman with a good figure and a pretty face. She was born in Segundo, Colorado, in 1902, in a boxcar that had been converted into the family home. Her mother died when she was a baby, and she was sent to Prescott, Arkansas, to be raised by her uncle Vernon and aunt Helen Poe Tompkins. Her father, E.E. Davis, was a man of many jobs, none of them steady. At one point he ran for local office on the Socialist ticket; this was before the Russian Revolution made Socialism a dirty word in America. Until then, it had had a rich history. I mention this because a strain of liberal, progressive worldview seeped through the generations and left its mark on me.

E.E. remarried and had four more children, two boys and two girls, but

Betty continued to live with Helen and Vernon in Prescott. Vernon was a respected lawyer whose partner, Thomas MacRae, would go on to serve as the governor of Arkansas. Helen, when she was younger, had written adventure stories for pulp magazines, earning as much as $500 per story. The Tompkinses were socially prominent in their small town; later, Betty would write that she felt "gauche" around a particular relative, a cousin by marriage who was even more of a Prescott "aristocrat" than her aunt and uncle. With Mary Anne, the black maid, doing most of the cooking and cleaning, Betty was spared the usual chores of childhood.

When she was in her mid-twenties and wanted to get away from home, Betty closed her eyes and put her finger on a map of the US. It landed on Wyoming, a state with ranches were so far-flung that instead of going to school, some children were taught by live-in teachers. Not knowing a single person in the entire state, Betty applied for a teaching position and was placed in the home of the Wright family. The parents were heavy drinkers with not a single cow on their "ranch." On weekends she flagged down the passenger train to hitch rides into town, and when the conductor threatened to put an end to these impromptu stops—according to him, each time it cost the railroad five dollars—Betty wrote to the railroad president. He wrote back, assuring her she could wave the train down as long as she liked. It continued to stop for her.

One school year on a ranch was enough. After Wyoming, Betty made her way back to Arkansas, where she taught for a year or two before moving to Chicago and enrolling at the American Academy of Arts on Wabash Avenue. She rented a room at the Green Gables Hotel, a rooming house on Lake Park Avenue close enough to feel the mist from Lake Michigan. The building was large, with seventy-five rooms and dozens of boarders. One of these was a young man named Ray Sabin.

Two years Betty's junior, Ray was a handsome California transplant with a motorcycle, a weekend job as a National Guardsman, and a steady job with a public utility company. He had grown up in Belvidere, Illinois, and then Los Angeles, where he graduated from high

*Four Sabin Brothers—Ray and Frank in rear,
Potter and David in front*

school. He briefly attended Lawrence College in Appleton, Wisconsin, not far from where one of his three brothers, my uncle Potter, served as a minister. When he was caught sharing test answers, he was asked to leave the college. He moved to Chicago and started working for Chicago Commonwealth Edison.

When my parents met around 1930, employment and a reliable paycheck were attractive qualities, especially for a woman wanting to start a family. Ray, though, wasn't much interested in tying himself down in marriage. Betty returned to Arkansas and her old beau Louie, a man she described as full of "sex appeal." But sex appeal wasn't much without a job; soon she was back in Chicago with Ray, who in the meantime had changed his mind about marriage. They wed in January of 1931.

My sisters, Nancy and Mimi, were six and four when I was born at the Chicago Lying-In Hospital on February 26, 1939. The first house I remember was one of a series of connected, two-story buildings on Plaisance Court at Blackstone and 59th Streets, on the city's South Side. The horseshoe-shaped development was fronted with a set of iron gates and located just off the Midway Plaisance, a mile-long grassy stretch that extended from Washington Park to Jackson Park, with a streetcar line that ended just outside Plaisance Court (the reason for all the clamor when the conductor flipped the seats).

The streets running alongside the parkway were heavily trafficked, but Blackstone itself was quiet. A half-block behind us on E. 60th Street, the St. George Hotel rose high above a strip of storefronts: the tailor's shop (exotic in our eyes because the tailor was Jewish); a drug store; the Van der Vort's grocery, where Mrs. Van der Vort and her daughter, Doris, lived in the back of the shop (Mr. Van der Vort was away at war). My sisters recall soaping the tailor's windows on Halloween; also, running along the halls of the St. George Hotel and joy riding in the elevator. My own memories are of clambering up mountains of coal stacked outside the University of Chicago's power plant and playing on the Midway, with its long lines of sailors drilling for the war overseas—a war we were suddenly pulled into with the bombing of Pearl Harbor when I was two.

The nearby Rosenwald Museum of Science and Industry fascinated me. They had everything from fetuses in glass jars to model electric trains. A simulated coal mine was in the basement. Seated in coal cars, you wound your way through cramped, dimly lit passageways with rough, dark walls and a low ceiling that curved just inches over your head. It was my favorite exhibit.

Outside were the Japanese gardens. That's where Nancy and her friend Marguerite Casper were standing when a man pulled down his pants. The experience taught us that adults sometimes behaved in odd ways.

I still remember some of my playmates. Whenever Patrick O'Malley came by, he stood outside and shouted, "Can Eddie come out, can Eddie come out?" He and I romped around the courtyard and in the nearby alleys, joined by Edwin and Arwin MacPherson and other neighborhood children. Carol MacPherson was a cute friend of Nancy's with blond Shirley Temple curls. She was my first crush.

Dad worked full-time at Commonwealth Edison on the night shift and took engineering classes part-time at the Armour Institute and Lewis Institute. At the substation he oversaw, he and another employee made rounds on catwalks above the huge inverters, monitoring gauges and recording data on charts. My mother's half-brother, Bill, came for a visit one night, and while Dad was giving him a tour of the facility, Bill reached up and pulled a lever. A section of Chicago was plunged into darkness. "Dropping the load," as it was known, could have cost Dad his job. He spent the rest of the shift doctoring the charts to hide the dip. Luckily, he was never found out.

Mother wasn't a natural-born housewife and didn't spend much time on cleaning, but she became a good cook, and Dad was home most evenings for supper. After the plates were cleared away, we listened as Dad read from favorite books: *Arabian Nights*, *The Travels of Ulysses*, Kipling's *Jungle Book*. When we were ready for bed, Mother took a turn reading to us in the living room.

Of our two parents, Dad was the more playful. He had a good sense of humor and a laugh like he was choking on a bone, although he generally kept both under wraps. Physically he tended to be aloof, just like his mother (according to my mother). Occasionally, though, he turned close contact into a game, like when he pulled his Laurel-and-Hardy move of squeezing through the doorway just as you were passing through it. He knew how to have fun with us in ways I didn't see with my friends' parents. For instance, he gave each of us a spoon and had us dig up dandelions from the Midway, then replant them on a bald patch of ground behind our house. He speculated that if grass wouldn't grow, maybe weeds would. (They didn't.) Some of his experiments were even stranger, like when he pushed a pin into his knee and encouraged Mimi to do so, too. "It's just pushing nerve cells aside," he explained. Mimi learned that pushing nerve cells aside hurt.

Once, Mother went away for an overnight trip and left Dad in charge. He saw no reason why the girls, including one of their little friends, shouldn't share the beer he was enjoying. They ended the evening with Mimi at the piano while Dad and the other girls marched around the room, waving little American flags and singing "The Star-Spangled Banana." Mother wasn't happy when she heard about it.

We didn't have any relatives in town, but our household expanded when Mother took in boarders. It may have been her interest in art that led her to offer a room to Mr. Reynolds, an artist, and to the widowed Mrs. Charles Abel Corwin, whose husband's dioramas were on display at the Field Museum. Another boarder worked in a classified A-bomb program that took place on the underground squash courts at the University of Chicago. The most memorable of the boarders, though, was Arlene Landry. Money was tight, and Mother had to take a job teaching school in Flossmoor, so she hired Arlene to be our babysitter. One weekend she left Arlene in charge while she was visiting family in Arkansas, and Arlene became catatonic. We kids looked on as she sat wordlessly, staring at the wall, until a paddy wagon came to take her away.

The war overseas gained momentum during the late 1930s, but many Americans were still convinced it would be a mistake for the United States to get involved. Memories of World War I, that supposed "War to End All Wars," were still fresh in the minds of people who had lived through it. Nobody wanted a repeat of those horrors.

That attitude changed overnight with the attack on Pearl Harbor. People pulled together to fight the German and Japanese menace, and patriotism ran high. Pacifism was dead, or nearly so. But not for my father. He remained staunchly anti-war. It's not that he wanted to avoid being in uniform; two of his older brothers had served in the Navy, and he had done his own stint with the National Guard. Besides, his work for a vital utility ensured that he wouldn't get called up. The issue went deeper than wanting to keep himself or other American soldiers out of harm's way; my dad was convinced of the immorality of war in general. It was a conviction he never gave up.

At home, life changed, though I was too young to have clear memories of it. I don't remember the rationing, except that people didn't drive much—gasoline purchases were restricted, as were the sale of new tires (most rubber was produced on Dutch East Indies plantations seized by the Japanese). People followed the progress of the war via radio reports, and, thanks to the movie newsreels and air transport, for the first time in history the public could see footage of battles soon after they occurred. Posters plastered on public walls and in shops encouraged people to buy war bonds, join the army, and recycle everything from metal to kitchen waste. Other placards whipped up patriotic fervor with sayings like, "We can do it!" and "Loose lips sink ships." "Kill the Germans" and "Kill the Japs" became common motifs in the comic books I loved to read, and movies carried the message even farther.

It wasn't just the outside world that was shifting; the winds of change were blowing for my family, too. Although Dad was well-suited to technical work, he had a curious mind and a strong sense of morality. At my mother's suggestion, they explored different religious denominations, searching for one they could practice together. It was Mother's idea to visit a Unitarian church in Chicago, where they met Ed Wilson, a minister and leader in the humanist movement. Wilson's preaching struck a chord with my father. He must have seen something in my dad, too. He encouraged him to return to college to become a Unitarian minister, advice my dad eventually took.

CHAPTER TWO

From Big City to Small Town

Dad finished his degree at the University of Chicago in 1941 and enrolled in Meadville Theological School. While my sisters and I were at school—first Ray School and then Scott School, where I finished first grade—Dad took day classes at Meadville and continued to work the night shift. It couldn't have been easy for Mother to keep us loud-mouthed kids quiet while he slept during the day. On Sundays, he took care of us while Mother taught Sunday school.

Dad graduated from Meadville in 1944. He "campaigned"—conducted services as a guest minister—while looking for a permanent position as a minister. He and my mother understood the financial ramifications of leaving Commonwealth Edison to enter the ministry. It was a leap of faith for both of them.

Family lore had it that our money troubles started after Dad quit the utility company, but that's probably not accurate. In Chicago there had been some money for extras, like my sisters' piano lessons. But even before my dad left for the ministry, he and my mother sat down every month at the dining room table to decide which bills to pay and which had to wait. They generally agreed on how to spend what they had, but something as simple as a car breakdown could cause a major problem. Of the two of them, my mother was by far the more practical-minded. Dad, by contrast, was the sort who didn't mind a bit of uncertainty, who assumed everything would work itself out. Today, I wonder about the strength it took for my mother to go along with some of his plans. As it turned out, giving up his annual $3,000 salary for an uncertain future was just the beginning.

After graduation, Dad was hoping for an appointment in the Midwest, but with more than half of the Unitarian congregations located in the East, he settled for a church in Mendon, Massachusetts. He was going from the hotbed of humanism in Chicago to a relatively staid and conservative congregation in semi-rural New England.

His new position wouldn't start until the fall of 1945, but by early summer that year we were on the train to Boston. The summer heat was oppressive, and hot cinders from the steam locomotive blew through the open windows and peppered our faces. From Boston, we left for Camp Chappa Challa on Cape Cod Bay, where Mother and Dad had jobs as camp counselors and my sisters and I attended camp alongside the children of wealthy New England families. We drove to the beach every afternoon, swinging our legs out the back of a slow-moving, wood-paneled station wagon.

Beautiful First Parish (Unitarian) Church, Mendon

That August, the Americans dropped atomic bombs on Hiroshima and Nagasaki, bringing World War II to a swift end. I don't remember the celebrations, but I've read about them in my father's journal. I'm sure he rejoiced that the war was over, but it came at a steep price: the dawn of the atomic age. While people shot off fireworks and honked their horns, he held a fast.

At the end of the summer, we moved to a cabin on Lake Nipmuc to wait until the Mendon parsonage was ready. The cabin was only a half-mile or so from town, but deep in nature and rudimentary, with no plumbing. During the day, we explored and swam in the lake; once a week, we took baths in a washtub filled with water heated on the stove.

We moved into the parsonage a month or so later. The two-story house was large but lacked modern amenities like plumbing and central heat. Uninsulated walls and single-pane windows made the high-ceilinged rooms drafty and cold. By our second year in the parsonage, the kitchen stove had been replaced with a modern range, and a coal-fired furnace had replaced the living room's wood stove. During that first winter, it was so cold that on some mornings a glass of water on the bedside table would be frozen solid. Dad's office with its smelly kerosene heater was the only room on the second floor with a source of heat.

It was in here that Dad composed his sermons. This dreaded task usually took place late Saturday night, after a week spent avoiding it. He would sharpen his pencils, brew a pot of coffee, and—finding no more excuses to procrastinate—sit down at his Underwood typewriter. On Sunday mornings, he woke with bags under his eyes, ready with a new sermon to deliver.

"I thought I heard the old man say, 'Leave her, Johnny, leave her.'" That line from an old sea chanty echoed through the house on Sunday mornings as Dad warmed up his voice before the service. Years later I recognized it as Dad giving voice to his unconscious wishes, a desire to leave behind all the family and ministerial responsibilities. He wore his life like a suit cut to fit someone else.

At Sunday school, the church was just as cold as the parsonage. Asa Vear, the old caretaker, had a funny notion that "you can't heat dead air," and insisted on opening all the windows before firing up the furnace. It took half the morning for the heat to beat back the cold. We spent Sunday school in our overcoats, not taking them off until the 11 a.m. service.

The parishioners welcomed us into their world. For my parents, the community spirit was a happy change from the impersonal atmosphere of Chicago. Cars were in short supply because of the war, and for the first couple of years, Dad relied on a maroon bicycle to ride up and down the hills of Mendon to call on church members. In 1947, we acquired a '31 Chevy.

Several people in the community pitched in to help modernize the parsonage. Putt Lowell, dairy store owner and head of the volunteer fire department, and Henry Clough, the school principal, spent several days with my dad digging up the yard for a septic system. Other work included pouring cement over the bare dirt floor in the basement, installing a coal furnace, and adding an indoor bathroom.

When we got the new kitchen range, Mother started baking cookies, cakes, and pies again. She was the cook and baker, and the rest of us, Dad included, helped with cleaning up. Milk was delivered from Lowell's dairy or Coffin's dairy. Coffin's bottles were fancier, with a round bulb-like top where cream collected.

Dad set up a workshop at the parsonage (he did this at every house we ever lived in). Boats were one of his fascinations. He had taken mechanical drawing in high school and had created skillful, detailed drawings of World War I cruisers and destroyers. Later, as an adult in Chicago, he built a two-foot-long, double-ended lifeboat modeled after one of the Coast Guard boats that chugged around Lake Michigan. The cabin housed a small, battery-powered motor and brass port lights, life lines, and a cockpit fore and aft.

His love of boats may have been inspired by two of his brothers, both in the Navy, or going further back, by his ancestor Edward Eels Potter. E.E. joined the Navy and fought in a Civil War battle aboard a Mississippi River gunboat; as captain of the USS *Constellation*, he brought relief provisions to Ireland during a famine; and he worked to recapture

American-owned ships from revolutionary fighters in South America. E.E. retired in 1895 with the title of commodore. He was something of a family hero.

Dad would become more anti-war and his workshop interests would shift to other subjects, but when I was young, he saw nothing wrong with me playing with toy soldiers. As a gift, I had received a lead soldier mold portraying five different World War I soldiers. Dad showed me how to melt lead in a tin can on my mother's stove and then pour the molten lead into the mold. It's a wonder I never burned myself.

In Mendon, Dad also helped me build a soapbox derby car for the annual race on the George Street hill. I was jealous when my friend Andy and his father showed up one year with a sleek derby car with expensive, low-friction wheels. By comparison, my car, constructed from a couple of two by fours and some baby buggy wheels, was crude. Then I saw the car Putt Lowell entered with his nephew, and I felt better. Putt was certain the small roller-skate wheels on their entry would win them the race, but Dad knew better. He predicted our car would go faster, and he was right. Andy won the race, but we beat the Lowells' car.

I was a good boy who didn't get into much trouble, but my sisters were older and bolder. Nancy seemed to be my father's favorite—she made herself more agreeable than Mimi did—but she liked boys and she liked staying out late, and that got her into trouble with my mother. Dad tended to stay out of it. I don't think conversing with young kids had much appeal for him, and disciplining us certainly did not.

I was like a little old man. When I walked into the darkened living room and discovered my sisters necking with boys, or caught them smoking cigarettes, I fretted about what it would do to their reputations. One time when they were sneaking a smoke in their bedroom, they threw a match into the trashcan and accidentally lit their curtains on fire. We had to call the fire department, which meant the whole town would know the preacher's girls were smoking. It was a relief when they spent summers away at a Unitarian work camp run by Paul and Marjorie Bliss, friends of my father. Nancy enjoyed the camp, but when it was Mimi's turn to go, she begged my parents to let her come home. It wasn't an option, however. Mother and Dad had closed up the parsonage for the summer, deposited me with one of the Mendon parishioners, and had taken temporary jobs at the state mental hospital in nearby Grafton.

In Chicago, our nearest relative had been Dad's older brother, Edward Potter Sabin, an Episcopal minister in Wisconsin and the source of my name. The second-born of the four Sabin boys, Uncle Potter was twelve years older than Dad and was his mentor. Most of Mother's family was down in Arkansas, and we never saw much of them, although after our move to New England, we were close enough to visit Aunt Julia Davis Millar in Claremont, New Hampshire. Aunt Julia was the product of my grandfather's second marriage and the younger of Mother's step-sisters. While she was working as a nurse in a hospital, Julia met a much older man, a patient who enjoyed her back rubs. They married and had four children, and when he died, he left her well taken care of. She took up politics and was elected to the New Hampshire Legislature, which she claimed was rife with corruption. She was a real character: a prosperous state rep who drank hard and never lost her Arkansas twang. Visits to her home were a treat.

I had already attended two schools by the time I completed first grade in Chicago, setting into motion an itinerant pattern that would continue throughout my life. In Mendon, there was one school for grades one through twelve. For two years starting in second grade, I had the misfortune of being taught by Mrs. Gaskill.

She was frightening. She was one of those old-school teachers who criticized not just schoolwork but also things like her students' posture. Similar to my father, I had a slight stoop, and no matter how many times Mrs. Gaskill told me to sit up, I soon slumped back into my usual posture. One day she got so aggravated that she

Grandmother Sabin, Ray, Ed, Nancy and Mimi in front of Mendon parsonage. Due to living in California, Grandmother Sabin rarely visited.

grabbed my ear and gave it a sharp tug. When I told my mother what had happened, she marched over to the school and had it out with Mrs. Gaskill, demanding that the teacher never lay a hand on me again. It was a confusing lesson about power and authority that left me puzzled. Here were two authority figures in my life, and they were clashing with one another. I was sorry my mother made an issue of it.

No less perplexing was my second-grade love life. I was shy, but not too shy to write love notes to Donna Vincent, the object of my affection. "I love you. Do you love me?" I scribbled on a piece of paper. However, in the note-passing shuffle to get it to her, the piece of paper was intercepted by another girl who read it and promptly agreed to be my girlfriend. I didn't care much for this second girl, but I didn't want to hurt her feelings, so I continued to write notes to both.

The Mendon school drew on the population from the surrounding area, and its atmosphere was warm and supportive. It had one large building with a playground out back; the principal, Mr. Clough, taught several classes. I was pals with Buster Miller, a rambunctious kid who lived in a small, kerosene-heated house on Washington Street across the pasture from the parsonage. His dad got interested in homing pigeons, and he showed us how to race them. Other friends were Andy Bowen, Gordon Harvey, and Charles Avery.

After school we roller-skated and played games like hide and seek and cops and robbers, or we went bike riding. I had to suffer the indignity of riding one of my sisters' bikes, as I wouldn't have my own until I earned the money to buy it a few years later. I rode with Buster as far as our energy would take us. We rode past the Piper Cubs parked on the small grass airfield and on to Lake Nipmuc; once or twice, we rode all the way to Bellingham, near the border with Rhode Island. I still recall the anxiety of sharing the narrow concrete road with big cement trucks.

Friction over money matters increased after our arrival in Mendon, when Dad's salary dropped from $3,000 to $1,800 per year. My mother brought in some money as a substitute teacher and we lived at the parsonage rent-free, but finances were tight. There were unexpected expenses, too, like the purchase of twenty-four new window curtains for the parsonage. Dad wrote to the Unitarian Association to plead for help: "We picked up some curtains at a rummage sale and were given some. As for shades, it is possible that the people here are waiting to see how much money will be left over after installing a bath and furnace." It's a common refrain in the life of a minister: relying on the largesse of the church community. It makes for an odd situation. As a minister, you're part of the middle class, expected by your church members to live accordingly, but you're not provided with a salary that allows you to do so. No wonder there was tension between my parents.

Any time one person is earning money (as Dad was doing) and the other is managing it (as Mother was doing), there is potential for trouble. Mother was a strong personality, and when she got angry at him, she didn't hold back. Her style was to argue loudly and volubly. In response, Dad would withdraw into silence. The further he retreated into himself, the louder she became. It didn't matter if the kids were around. "You don't earn enough for us," she ranted, or, "Why are we so poor?" He would strike back in some passive-aggressive manner, giving her the silent treatment or using phrases such as "you're wacky" instead of "you're welcome" or "shoot yourself" instead of "suit yourself." It set up a pattern that I tried to avoid later in life when I married.

I do recall one occasion when Dad spent money they probably couldn't afford. When I was seven or eight, my sisters and I were warned to keep our expectations low for Christmas, because, as usual, there wasn't much money. I'd been eyeing a couple of Lionel train sets at the toy store in Milford. One model featured a streamliner locomotive, but I preferred the less expensive set with its older-style steam engine. Still, I knew it wasn't likely I'd see anything so costly under the tree. That's why I was surprised on Christmas morning when I woke up to find the streamliner model waiting for me. We set it up on a large piece of plywood and each year added new cars with more track and switches. I never did mention to my dad that it wasn't the one I wanted.

In some ways, Dad was ahead of his time. When I was a young man in the 1960s, you could find plenty of people—myself included—turning our backs on the live-to-work mentality of our parents' generation, when a man's primary goal in life was to work hard to support his family. Dad threw out that notion years before the social convulsions of the 1960s. Financial security wasn't the North Star by which he guided his life; he believed in searching for a deeper, more meaningful path. What makes life worth living? What are the big questions, and how are they to be answered? Those were the questions that drove him.

Mother, on the other hand, was keenly aware that it took a steady income to raise three children; in bad times, she and Dad sometimes had to borrow my sisters' babysitting money. To ease the strain, Mother worked for a year as a teacher in West Upton.

As a family, we were well established in the Mendon community. My sisters and I had our school friends, and our parents were busy tending to the church community, overseeing everything from summer camps to Sunday school. Our family was involved with the Unitarian Service Committee that collected clothing and supplies for the refugees and displaced persons set adrift by the war. Dad was a volunteer firefighter, and I recall him jumping out of bed at the first wail of the fire alarm. More often than not, it was a brush fire. But while the town had opened its arms to us, we—or rather my parents—remained to some extent outsiders. This showed up in subtle and not so subtle ways.

Mother had grown up in the Jim Crow South. She didn't know it at the time, but even her uncle, the man she called "Daddy," was a member of the Ku Klux Klan. She had unknowingly witnessed his arrival with fellow Klansmen at the funeral of a town marshal who'd been shot for destroying a bootlegger's still. Years later, she discovered his white robe and hood in a box. Racial hatred was as much a part of her heritage as was a Southern twang, and she successfully shed both as an adult. She once told me that the years of being married to my father had helped rub off the more egregious expressions of her Southern prejudice, although some wisps of it remained, as it does for most Americans. In Mother's case, it wasn't so much a matter of race but of class.

Byron and George Haywood were from a poor family in Mendon. "Byron Haywood, that sounds like such a classy name, doesn't it?" she'd say, trying to see beyond the boys' choppy, homespun haircuts and dirty necks. The tall, thin brothers were aloof and proud. When Mimi decided she wanted to convert our old outhouse into a laboratory for her collection of animal bones, Mother hired Byron to shovel it out; in a strange mixture of condescension and compassion, she then persuaded him afterward to take a bath in our new bathroom.

In our small, conservative New England town, Dad earned the reputation of a left-wing liberal. He was a vocal advocate of the United Nations from its earliest days, when many still viewed the new institution with suspicion; he handed out Planned Parenthood literature at the polling place; and when a single vote was cast for Henry Wallace, the Progressive Party candidate in the 1948 presidential election, it wasn't hard for the people of Mendon to figure out whose vote it was.

During a minstrel show put on by the fire department in the town hall, the performers gently poked fun at my dad. "Reverend Sabin, are those pickles in your package?" one character asked. The man playing my father held a paper sack that was visibly leaking. "No," came the response, "they're puppies." The sketch drew guffaws from the audience, but Dad wasn't there to hear them. He was opposed to minstrel shows in general and had avoided attending by volunteering to man the fire station that evening. My sister Mimi doesn't agree with me, but my theory is that he skipped it because he found minstrel shows racially offensive. This was the man who protested when Louis McGee, an African American Unitarian minister, couldn't find a church; the man who taught us to sing along to "Little Songs on Big Subjects" ("Oh, ho, ho, can't you see, the color of your skin doesn't matter to me..."); the man who encouraged Mimi to play those same songs during a church revue. How could he be expected to watch a group of men in blackface tell jokes in a mangled black accent? Simple. He couldn't.

Maybe the congregation would have forgiven their minister for his liberal ideas if he had kept them to himself. But my dad couldn't do that either. His sermons brimmed over with the issues that concerned him: social equity, injustice, the dangers of preparing for another war. He continued to study and learn from other people who grappled with the same questions, philosophers and theologians who looked beyond the Bible for answers.

Not everyone was disenchanted with my dad. Years later Andy Bowen wrote to tell me that his father and mother had become lifelong Unitarians (later morphing into atheists) because of my parents' influence. But in the end, Dad's sermons alienated too many church members. So did his rather formal manner. Had he been more of a hail-fellow-well-met, he might have found more sympathy among parishioners. As it was, each week church attendance fell. Where there were once seventy or more people in the congregation, by the late 1940s fewer than half that number attended church regularly. Thirty people sitting spread out in church is a disheartening sight. Our mother insisted we be there to swell the crowd. Unfortunately, as time went on, there was no crowd to swell.

Four years after taking over the Mendon pulpit, Dad wrote in his journal: "Only a handful in church and I thought perhaps I ought to resign now instead of August..." As it turned out, he waited until the summer break before we packed up and headed for Peabody, Massachusetts. In August 1949, he was installed as the new minister of Peabody's Park Street Church.

CHAPTER THREE

Peabody

Mendon was a largely Protestant town, small and semi-rural; Peabody, by comparison, was full of working-class Irish and Italian Catholics and had the feel of a bustling city. The tanneries that had given Peabody its nickname, "Leather City," also gave it its trademark smell. Fortunately, after a while you didn't notice.

Our house at 26 Emerson Street was in a quiet neighborhood about a mile from the church. Behind the house was a cinder-block garage and a large apple tree; this was where you'd typically find our old Chevy parked (the axle broke often, and there were long periods of waiting until we had the money to fix it). In Mendon, we had either burned garbage or thrown it onto the compost heap, but in Peabody there was an underground receptacle next to the back stoop, designed with a lid flush to the ground that opened with a foot pedal. A few steps farther was the domain of boys all over American cities: the alleyway. It was here, at the far end of the block, in front of a shed flanked by shrubs, that my friends and I gathered to talk about girls, argue about religion (I was the sole Protestant among Catholics), and see who could pee the farthest. We roamed the town and stayed out late on summer evenings. Sometimes we crossed the railroad tracks and climbed a granite cliff, clinging to narrow ledges in an old quarry.

I started sixth grade at Center School, a good school with fine teachers. I especially liked Miss Billings, the English teacher who taught us how to diagram sentences. All my friends from the neighborhood, like Dickie and Jimmy Connolly and Eddie Donovan, went next door at St. John the Baptist School. During recess, I marveled at the nuns in their long black habits who kept watch over their students. They looked scary.

The Connollys lived three doors from us. At home we listened to the radio for entertainment—a favorite was the "Bob and Ray" show broadcast out of Boston—but Mr. Connolly was a lawyer for the Harvard Beer Company, and they had a television set. Jimmy Connolly was closest to my age, but it was his younger brother Dickie who became my best friend. I recall going with Dickie to gather empty soda bottles after social events in the basement of the Park Street Church, then collecting the two-cent deposit for each bottle at the grocery store. We would use the money to buy eclairs and cream puffs at a nearby French Canadian bakery.

Mother usually bought groceries from the A&P, but occasionally she sent me to pick up something from Champaign's Grocery Store. If she gave me cash, I was allowed to buy penny candy with the change, such as licorice sticks or miniature wax "soda bottle" candy, but that didn't happen often. Champaign's, which was more expensive than the A&P, allowed customers to buy on credit. If Mother sent me there, it usually meant we were low on money that month.

When I was younger we'd had a mixed-breed dog named Pootsie, but in Peabody our family dog was a dachshund mix named Weenie. Years earlier my father had drowned a litter of kittens, an ordeal he vowed never to repeat, so when Weenie went into heat, we locked her in the basement, and it was my job to clean up her messes. The smell was awful.

Mimi had been playing the piano since she was a young girl, and Mother managed to scrape together enough to continue her lessons in Peabody. Dad thought it was time she started on some Bach, and the instructor agreed, but she started her on a book of music that was too advanced. Mimi complained, and the piano lessons ended.

Ed with Wienie and tugboat model on the back porch of Peabody parsonage. Ray built the model from scratch. Powered by lead acid batteries, it was powerful enough to pull a person on an inner tube.

Like they'd done in Mendon, the parishioners in Peabody were kind to us and helped out by passing along hand-me-downs. I didn't mind it because we needed the stuff. I got a nice coat from the Sargents, and a stack of adventure war stories by R. Sydney Bowen from the Blisses. One series featured teenaged hero Dave Dawson battling enemies during World War II: *Dave Dawson at Dunkirk, Dave Dawson in Libya, Dave Dawson at Singapore,* and a dozen more. Another was the Red Randall series. I inhaled them all. By this time the war had been over for five years but still lived on in my imagination. I loved comic books that featured World War II stories with all the guns, tanks, ships, and planes. Inspired, I spent countless hours drawing pictures of tanks, ships, and planes. The history and technology of the war fascinated me.

When I was about twelve, I got my first job as a newspaper boy. At first I had only a few customers, but after I bought a route from an older boy, the number increased to about forty. I delivered several Boston morning papers, including the *Globe*, the *Record*, and the *Herald*. Within a few months, my route had grown to about fifty houses. Boy, that was something; for the first time ever, I had good money.

However, I didn't enjoy collecting it from customers. Each week, I had to knock on doors and ask for payment. Sometimes someone would hold out for a few weeks, which made it uncomfortable for both of us.

Still, the experience taught me good business lessons and I liked other aspects of working the route, even getting up at 5:00 or 5:30 a.m. On winter mornings, my footprints were the first in the fresh snow as I passed by the school and the ballfields on the mile-long walk to the pickup office downtown. I waited with other paperboys for the truck that came in daily from Boston, carrying five or so different newspapers. We stood together as we folded our papers and shoved them into our canvas sacks. Weekdays were easy, but the weekend edition was fatter and heavier. Nobody used rubber bands. We had a special technique of rolling it from one side and folding it into a sort of pocket on the other side. If you pressed down hard, it would hold. Then I hauled the heavy sack over my shoulder and went to work, keeping track of which houses took which paper. I had a good number of customers, but my route was more spread out than most.

On my thirteenth birthday, I got my first bicycle. I paid for most of it with money I had earned on the paper route, with some chipped in by my family. The new Indian bicycle was beautiful, with three speeds and thin, sleek tires. It was imported from England, where bikes were still regarded as a means of transportation rather than a form of recreation. No more girl's bike with fat balloon tires for me. With the new bike, I could ride as far as I pleased.

My dad wasn't the kind to toss a ball around with me; neither of us was much interested in sports (I was the kid who was often picked last for a team), but in Peabody he did allow me to join him in some of his workshop projects. Working with his hands was a form of recreation for him, a way to combine his practical know-how and his creativity. Sometimes it also engaged his imagination, as with his model boats: He sometimes described himself as a frustrated sailor with dreams of sailing off to the South Seas to live on the beach with dancing girls.

He didn't teach me skills outright. For instance, with woodworking, he would give me a tip or two, but mostly he was content to let me learn by observing. He wasn't a fine woodworker and had no interest in creating things like dovetail joints, but he had a good sense of how to make something that would perform well. He valued quality. If my own efforts fell short, I soon learned, he would let me know. One example: When I built a nightstand for him and my mother, he pointed out all its defects. I remember it hurt my feelings, but I also recall how much the nightstand wobbled.

When I was in the sixth or seventh grade, Dad was inspired to build a model tugboat sturdy enough to tow a person on an inner tube. First, he needed to see real life examples. He took me out of school for the day, and we drove into Boston, where he photographed the tugboats chugging around the harbor. In his mind, this was a worthy educational outing. My teacher didn't agree.

In the basement workshop, I watched the new tugboat take shape under his hands. Working without a pattern, he cut oval shapes out of three-quarter-inch planks, making each slightly larger than the previous. Then he glued them on top of one another. Peering inside the boat, you could see the gradation from one piece to the next, but the exterior was planed down to create a smooth hull. Waterproof glue wasn't readily available, so he made his own by dissolving objects made of celluloid—a roll of film, a kewpie doll—in a jar of acetone. When it was finished, the tugboat measured almost three feet long and had a battery-powered propeller. It could tow an inner tube, although I don't know if it ever managed to pull a person on a tube.

It was around this time that Dad taught me and Dickie how to build a cannon. We started by making a solid, six-inch clay cannon model. We set this in a cigar box and poured plaster of paris around it, creating a mold in two pieces. Next, we melted down my toy soldiers and poured the molten lead into the mold. When it hardened, my dad helped us bore out the center and add a touch hole. In the end, we had a functioning, six-inch cannon.

The next step was making gunpowder. I'm not sure if my father gave us the formula, or if we looked it up in an encyclopedia. One of the ingredients was potassium chlorate, which you might have trouble finding at a store today, but back then people gargled with it, so it was easy to buy at the drugstore. As an active oxidizing agent, it wasn't as stable as potassium nitrate (otherwise known as saltpeter), but it was easier to ignite. We had to be careful when we mixed it with sulfur and charcoal, because even a slight amount of friction could set the whole thing off. The experience of playing with gunpowder may have influenced Dickie's decision later to become a pharmacist.

It didn't take much powder to blow a marble high into the air. But after a few shots, the burning powder melted the touchhole and made it so wide that the charge inside would fizzle without any explosion. That's when Dickie and I improvised with two-by-four and four-by-four pieces of wood. We used a brace and bit to drill out a "barrel" in the wood, drilled a smaller touch hole from the top, poured in homemade gunpowder, and packed it with dirt and gravel so tightly that it didn't have a chance of blowing out when we lit the powder. Instead, the explosion shattered the wood with a big, satisfying bang. We were fortunate not to injure ourselves.

My mother disapproved of guns but reluctantly agreed to let me buy a .22 rifle from a friend when I was twelve. My dad instructed me on gun safety, something he'd learned from his time in the National Guard. We shot tin cans in the woods, or in the shooting range Dad set up in the basement, with scrap wood attached to the home's stone foundation. When you hit a tin can full of water—our usual target—with a .22 short, the can danced around and shot water everywhere. My mother wasn't too happy about it, but for my dad and me, it was great fun.

In Peabody, my sisters worked part-time jobs and belonged to the Unitarian youth group. Mimi made the cheerleading squad and was voted prettiest girl in school. I was looking forward to starting high school, too. I had friends, and things were going well for me. In eighth grade, a student set fire to Center School, and the old brick building burned furiously. I thought that would be the end of school for the year, but we ended up going half-days at another school some distance away.

My father continued to walk his own path; the experience in Mendon hadn't dulled his need to push for change and seek answers to life's bigger questions. He was still an optimist, always cultivating faith in human nature. Here's just one example: While we were away for two weeks, he deliberately left our house unlocked, and when nobody broke in, he took it as proof that people are basically good.

However, the people of Peabody were losing sympathy with him as a minister. Churchgoers didn't want to hear his views on the United Nations, or about the dangers of another world war, or about his annual letter to the governor of Massachusetts protesting Spanish-American War celebrations (the governor proclaimed the war as "a great armed crusade of the American people for world freedom;" Dad saw it differently). His flock wanted religion, not politics. Sunday attendance dwindled.

Maybe that's the reason he was so receptive to a talk he heard in the spring of 1952. He and Mother drove to Haverhill to attend a slideshow presentation by Hardy Arnold, one of the leaders of the Bruderhof, a religious community founded thirty years earlier by Hardy's father, Eberhard Arnold. My dad was struck by Hardy's description of six hundred people living together in a remote corner of Paraguay, working together and sharing goods in common.

Europe has a long tradition of Christian socialism, but in the US, socialism has always been a strictly secular movement. With the Bruderhof, the secular and Christian overlapped where it most counted with Dad: in their denunciation of war, and in their faith in non-violence, internationalism, and men and women working for the common good. Dad met resistance in Peabody for simply wanting to fly the United Nations flag. Hardy Arnold, by contrast, described a seemingly idyllic settlement where people of all nationalities lived, ate, and worked together. Dad's journal entry mirrored his immediate enthusiasm: "Apparently they practice what we preach. We want in!" In a later letter, he explained that after years of skidding between "agnosticism, atheism, humanism, and naturalism," he was ready to have a go at "traditional theology."

I don't recall when it dawned on me that we were headed for another big change. I was thirteen and more interested in girls and my friends than the German man in homespun clothing who came to visit my parents. Dad invited Hardy and Leonard Pavitt, another member and fellow fund-raiser, to talk to his congregation about the Bruderhof. My mother, always the more practical of my parents, wasn't as enthralled as Dad, but Hardy had caught her attention, too. She had an adventurous streak.

Over next few months, discussions gave way to plans, and plans resolved into action. We were moving to South America. By June 1952, my dad had resigned his ministry and we had sold or given away most of our belongings, including our dog Weenie. I don't remember having positive or negative feelings about our upcoming move. I was fine going along with the program, ready to go with the family wherever they wanted to go.

That summer, Nancy worked in Peabody at a law office, and Mimi was invited to stay with her boyfriend, Bob Locke, and his parents while she waited tables at the House of Seven Gables in Salem. I joined my parents at Morgan Goodwill Camp, a summer camp for inner-city kids run by Goodwill Industries, where they worked as camp counselors. A girl whose name I can't remember became my first girlfriend.

Dad was put in my building with the boy campers, and Mother was housed some distance away with the girl campers. Another married couple, also counselors, lived in our building, and Dad and the woman became attracted to each other. Of course I didn't know anything about it until years later; my sisters and I also learned that the woman had a pattern of carrying on these kinds of flirtations.

She and my dad passed his journal back and forth, writing entries for each other to read. The relationship nearly ended my parents' marriage. Fortunately at the end of summer and after some rocky sessions between my mother and dad, the flirtation ended.

CHAPTER FOUR

Journey to Paraguay

It's pretty clear my father's troubles with the congregations in Mendon and Peabody increased his desire to run off to South America to visit the Bruderhof. It would be a fresh start, a chance to escape the frustrations of preaching messages people did not want to hear. What's remarkable is that he chose to throw in his lot with a group that included some fundamentalists. He shared the same value system of working for the greater good, but he tended more towards humanism than theism. In one of his sermons, he preached, "Modern religion says that the final responsibility is upon man himself, if he would have a longer, richer, more peaceful life. Our destiny lies in our own hands—none other." That was a world away from the message of the Bruderhof.

Years later, I would have a conversation with my dad and his friend, Wally Bush, at my parents' home in Idaho Springs, Colorado. Wally's orthodox approach to sin would shock me, but reflecting back on it, I think it was an attitude my father probably shared. "Sin" was a word you rarely heard among Unitarians, but Wally defended the concept.

"I'm a sinner," he said. "And unless one is laboring under the liberal belief in the perfectibility of human beings—and the 20th century and World War II with its fifty million dead should have dispelled that goofy notion—there's nothing wrong with admitting to being a sinner. Sin is part of being human. Saints are those who live for others in a way that most of us can't (or won't) do. We're all sinners," Wally wrote. If my dad felt this way, too, it would have been another reason the Bruderhof appealed to him. Here were humans who had the audacity to live with one another like brothers and sisters, or at least try to.

Money remained a frequent topic of conversation, only now that we were older, everyone was involved. We kids weren't shielded from the trouble money—or rather, the lack of it—caused; we knew how much it cost to fix the Chevy or when Mother and Dad visited the loan company or put in a call to Aunt Julia. Maybe this openness, this practice of making money a family issue, is why we took a team attitude toward earning the money needed for our trip to South America.

At the end of the summer, my parents and sisters moved to Westboro, Massachusetts, to work at the state hospital, and I was left in the care of Gladys Morrison, a friend of my mother who lived on Providence Road in Mendon. My parents reasoned that it was better for me to start ninth grade in familiar surroundings rather than start a new school in Westboro, particularly since we didn't expect to be in the US for much longer.

Mrs. Morrison gave me an attic bedroom and offered me fifty cents an hour to paint their garage. I told her I'd do it for twenty-five cents and then did very little of the work, partly because the pay was so low, then felt guilty about it afterward. At school, I took French with Mr. Clough. I thought I could read through the textbook and call it done; I was surprised he actually expected me to memorize French vocabulary. It was a valuable lesson I later put to use when studying other foreign languages.

Some of the kids took turns making out behind the church building after youth group meetings, but I didn't have my first physical experience with a girl until that fall, when I went to a sock hop in someone's garage. "Shine On, Harvest Moon" played on the record player as I danced with Donna Vincent, the same girl I had passed notes to in second grade. She had developed by this point, and I was thrilled to hold her close. I was certain someone would step in and break it up, but no one did. At the end of the evening, singing the lyrics to "Walking My Baby Back Home," I walked Donna home. My friend Andy walked with Shirley, Donna's neighbor. Later that fall I dropped by Donna's house for a visit and found her in overalls and rubber boots, shoveling manure in the cow barn. I wanted to tell her I thought she was just as pretty as she'd been at the dance, but I didn't. She never forgave me for seeing her like that.

That fall, I made frequent visits to the library and read a lot. I missed my family. My parents must have recognized how lonely I was without them; a month or two later, they moved into a larger three-room apartment in Westboro, near Lyman Street and the Worcester Boston Turnpike, and brought me to live with them.

I continued with ninth grade in Westboro and got a part-time job disbudding carnations at the McGuffie Greenhouse for fifty cents an hour. The flowers grew in four-foot-wide trays set on long tables that stretched the length of the greenhouse, and my task was to pluck the small buds off the plants. At home, I read a lot and built at least a half-dozen model airplanes, World War II fighter planes made from balsa sticks and paper with wingspans of nearly a foot and a half. I hung them from the apartment ceiling.

By May, we had saved enough to cover the cost of passage to South America. We sold our '39 Chevy for thirty-five dollars and filled four fifty-five-gallon drums with everything we were leaving behind and stored them in the basement of the church organist. If we decided to make the move a permanent one, she could have them shipped to us later. She also agreed to take our dog Wienie. My dad gave away the family's model boats, and I was told to get rid of my model airplanes. Shooting a rubber band slingshot loaded with pieces of lead from empty tubes of airplane glue, I pretended I was firing anti-aircraft shells; the "artillery" tore through the paper and balsa wood. I burned what was left in the backyard.

On Monday, May 4, 1953, at a quarter past five in the morning, we climbed into a vehicle owned by the Bruderhof and departed Massachusetts. With fifty pieces of luggage packed onto a trailer behind us (our belongings plus supplies for the Bruderhof), travel was slow. The heavy trailer weaved back and forth in the wind; outside of Camden, New Jersey, where we picked up Hardy's brother and sister-in-law, Heini and Annemarie Arnold, we had a blowout. The rest of the 1,500-mile trip to Miami passed without incident.

By midnight, I was excited to be on my first airplane, an old four-engine that delivered us, seven and a half hours later, to Tocumen, Panama. At the airport, we were met by Jim Bernard, a Bruderhof member who, along with his wife and mother, would accompany us to Paraguay. Jim spoke Spanish, a language none of my family knew.

We checked into the Hotel Central in the old center of Panama City to wait for our ship. Across the square was the Cathedral Basilica of St. Mary, a beautiful structure dating back to the 1600s. At night, flocks of blackbirds descended into the trees on the square and set up a terrible racket. Our hotel had high ceilings, good food, and shutters that let the breeze in but kept the hot sun out. We explored the city and tasted our first mangoes, papayas, and plantains. At the pool, I ran into a friend from Mendon, and he and I went to the movies.

After a week in Panama City, the *Amerigo Vespucci* arrived. The combined freighter and passenger ship was making its way down the western coast of South America, picking up and dropping off passengers, delivering cargo or loading it—primarily bananas—for the trip back to Europe. We traveled third-class, my mother and the girls in one cabin (the "nicer" one) and my dad and I in another. Red wine and hard rolls accompanied every meal but breakfast. I thought it was great.

Over the next month of travel, everything was new and different, and sometimes a little scary. After crossing the Panama Canal, we made several stops, including at Buenaventura, Colombia; Callou, Peru; and Arica, Chile. We made daylong excursions to see the ports of call, but most of our time was spent on the ship. Mrs. Bernard gave my dad lessons in German, Mimi studied Spanish, and my dad worked with me on algebra. It's difficult to have a parent as your teacher; it seemed to me like he was making up arbitrary algebra rules. Both of us ended up feeling frustrated.

When we crossed the Equator, my dad took photographs and my mother and I shot off fireworks. Peddlers came on board at Guayaquil, Ecuador. A passenger fell overboard after a night on the town and was swept away by a strong tide. There was no rescue attempt.

Our ship's journey came to an end at Antofagasta, Chile. We lugged our fifty bags through customs and to the train station, where we bought tickets for four cabins, one entire train car. The narrow-gauge railway climbed up to the Argentine border, where we waited for a couple of hours at the foot of the snow-capped peak of Socompa (elevation 19,700 feet) for our next train, the *General Belgrano*. We weren't as lucky this time. The cars were all open seats, and the train stopped frequently to let on more passengers. We pulled out blankets to keep warm as the train crossed the Andes through the night, and in the morning, the windows were heavily frosted. We had climbed 13,000 feet before descending.

In Salta, Jim Bernard tried to chase down some Argentinian currency to pay for our hotel and meals. There was some trouble with customs about the luggage, and we missed the next twice-weekly train on our itinerary. I didn't mind the delay. I had found a roadside cart that sold slices of cheese and tomato pizza, something I'd never tasted before. It was wonderful. It didn't cost much, so I kept going back to our hotel for more money to buy more slices. I don't remember if I let the rest of the party in on the bonanza. I also had my first cup of yerba mate in Salta, a drink that was a staple at the Bruderhof.

The next train ride took us to Embarcación, where we spent the night

Ed standing beside General Belgrano train high in the Andes near the border of Chile and Argentina

in a hotel. Hanging on the hotel room wall was a picture of St. Roque, along with a prayer for protection against bugs. It didn't work. "I'd rather spray than pray," my mother said.

After another train ride to Formosa, we switched to a bus. The road was muddy and slow-going, and at one point another bus had to attach a rope and pull us out of the mud. We made it to Clorinda in time to catch the ferry across the Paraguay River to Asunción, the capital of Paraguay. We were officially greeted by several members of the community and brought to Bruderhof House. The building was part administrative office, part way station for travelers going to and from the more distant Bruderhof villages, and part showroom for beautiful native hardwood wooden cups and bowls made in one of the villages. Collectively known as Primavera, the Bruderhof villages were located fifty miles upriver and thirty miles inland. We enjoyed a big lunch and spent the evening sitting around, singing and telling stories.

The next day, my sisters and I boarded a riverboat with Jim Bernard and his wife, leaving my parents and Jim's mom behind to get the bags through customs before they completed the trip to Primavera on a small plane. Our group slept on the riverboat that night as it chugged its way up the Paraguay River, and the next day in Rosario, we climbed onto a horse-drawn wagon for the final thirty miles to the Bruderhof. That doesn't sound far, but the mud was two feet deep in some places. We pitched camp in the open air, built a fire, and sang songs, and the next day, on our final leg of the voyage, a Mennonite family fed us lunch. It was the first time I ever ate black bean soup. At four in the afternoon on June 4, we arrived at the Loma Hoby, one of the three villages of Primavera. The next day, we were joined by our parents.

Sabin Family in Primavera. Back: Ray and Betty; front, left to right: Mimi, Ed, Nancy

CHAPTER FIVE

The Bruderhof

Primavera is an estancia or ranch bought in 1940 by the Society of Brothers. The Society of Brothers was founded in 1920 by Eberhard Arnold in Germany in the ferment following World War I. With the rise of Hitler, the community migrated to Switzerland and then to England. At the beginning of World War II, the community was expelled from England for refusing to send their German members away. Only Paraguay was willing to accept the community. Mennonites who settled in Paraguay near Primavera helped the community in the early years. The first village built at Primavera was named Isla Margarita. They lived for some time in shelters of boxes, crates, and canvas while they cleared land and put up houses. Since then two more villages have been built: Loma, a center for cattle ranching and the location of the hospital; and Ibaté, now the principal farming village.

—from a newsletter written by my dad, Ray Sabin

I was glad to finally arrive after our long month of traveling. Our new home was located in a land of *campos*, a sea of rough grassland dotted with islands of semi-tropical forests on higher, more fertile land. The

At home in Ibaté: The guest house where Ray, Betty, and Ed lived for about 4 months in 1953. Note peanut roasting oven at our feet, built by Ed and Peter Trapnell.

Bruderhof, which had originally occupied a piece of land in the harsh Chaco region of Paraguay, had cleared some of the forested ground and built its three villages here, each about a quarter of a mile long.

When we arrived, residents poured into the common area of the *Hof* (the German word used for the villages) to greet us with song and handshakes. I was impressed and a little overwhelmed. Mother, Dad, and I were given a gnome-like, two-room cottage in Ibaté, and my sisters were assigned lodgings a couple of miles away, at Loma. Our cottage was one of the single houses reserved for guests, but in every other way it resembled the duplexes where the permanent residents lived: thatched roof, clay floor, and walls made of split palm trunks, plastered with clay and white-washed. Mother and Dad slept in the back room, and I slept in the living room/kitchen area. We were given a few metal plates and some silverware, and a basin and jug for washing up. There was no sink or plumbing; after you washed up, you threw the dirty water outside. The outdoor privy was around the corner, some distance away, and near that was a cold-water shower.

There was an effort at the time to align with an Anabaptist group in Canada and North Dakota, and the Bruderhof's clothing as a result had grown more conservative. There were no buttons—too fancy—and the women all wore matching kerchiefs with white polka dots on a blue background. The clothes in the community were sewn from large bolts of cloth, so often women's and girl's dresses matched. Typical footwear consisted of a pair of wooden clogs with a leather strap, good for navigating the mud after it rained. For the first few months, I wore the clothes I had brought with me (including underwear, which prompted teasing by the other kids, who wore none), then switched to the home-sewn trousers and shirts worn by the other boys. When our clothes wore out, we were issued new ones.

All items were owned in common, and there was no exchange of money in the community (some younger members had never seen money). Toiletries, clothes, and breakfast food were parceled out to each family from the storehouse. Breakfast and tea were the only meals eaten at home with your own family. Each week we were given a loaf of hefty brown bread, jam or molasses, a jar of runny lard with a cap to keep the flies out, and mate, a traditional herbal drink in Paraguay.

The baker, Joseph Staegnl, lived and worked across from our hut in Ibaté, and I had the chance to observe the baking process. With wheat shipped from overseas and an industrial mixer (one of the few electric appliances in the hof), he and his young helper poured batter into large baking pans and baked them in a brick wood-fired oven. After the loaves cooled, they sewed them into large white cotton bags to be delivered by wagon to the other hofs.

Noontime dinner and evening supper took place in the community hall, a large, open-airbuilding with long tables and backless benches. Food was passed around in large enamel bowls, and everyone served himself. Utensils were simple metal bowls, spoons, and a drinking cup for yerba mate or water. Boiled mandioca, a white tuberous vegetable also known as cassava or manioc, was the base for most communal meals. The tuber is roughly the shape of a long sweet potato, about one to two feet long and two or three inches in diameter. Sometimes it was served topped with a kind of goulash of beef and gravy. Basins of the meat and gravy were passed down the communal table, with each person ladling as much as he wanted. Mandioca also showed up most nights in the form of a dessert called *schlempe*. The gelatin-like dish was made with mandioca starch and either the roselle plant or juice from bitter oranges. The more I ate *schlempe*, the less I liked it. I never understood why the brothers cultivated bitter orange trees instead of the sweet orange trees that seemingly grew wild in the forest. Maybe it was because the latter were so tall that you had to pick the fallen fruit off the ground or have someone climb up and throw the oranges down. They tasted wonderful.

Other than some dried sausage and the pieces of meat swimming in the goulash, we did not eat much meat; I don't remember any bacon, ham, or other breakfast meat at Primavera. Every now and then we would be treated to a feast of deep fried pig bones (mostly vertebrae). The skinny Paraguayan cows didn't produce much milk, and what they did was usually reserved for pregnant women, young children, and sick people. It was poured into small aluminum pails, covered with a cloth, and set into a basin of water to keep it cool. With no refrigeration, it didn't keep long. Eggs also weren't common. Occasionally you'd get one as a treat, but mostly they were reserved for the sick or the elderly, who ate at separate tables in the dining hall. They received somewhat better food than the rest of us: white bread instead of brown bread, butter instead of pig fat, sweetened cream of wheat instead of *schlempe*.

In contrast to the bland food, the singing and talking at communal meals was notable. People spontaneously broke into song—usually a German hymn—and others would join in. When we weren't singing, someone was talking. Visitors stood up to tell their life story, individuals read letters from abroad, and reports were given about news from the outside world, with translations from German into English and, occasionally, Spanish. I enjoyed listening to the life stories, something people also did while visiting each other during afternoon teatime. It's a kind of sharing we don't do much in this country.

The community hall was also the site for meetings. Prayer meetings took place on Sunday mornings and after some of the evening meals.

They ran long and could be boring, especially as we didn't understand German. One time I happened to be in front of the speaker and I got so sleepy I couldn't keep my eyes open. It was tough. Other meetings we as visitors were not invited to attend; we were curious about what went on during those members-only sessions.

The three hofs—Ibaté, Loma Hoby, and Isla Margarita—were all roughly two miles apart. The community owned a couple of British military trucks for hauling supplies from Rosario, but almost all travel was done on foot or by horse- or ox-drawn wagon. Boys as young as eight rode bareback, and girls the same age drove teams. Many kids jogged around on little gray burros.

The wagon wheels were wood rimmed with steel, and they cut deep ruts into the clay roads. Someone, possibly a foreign aid program, brought in bulldozers and built a new road that stretched a few miles outside of Rosario, although it stopped short of Primavera. The authorities didn't want the new road getting rutted, so we were forbidden to run wagons on it when the weather was wet. That caused a curious sight: the new road, framed on either side by parallel sets of deep ruts where the wagons drove.

During big celebrations, everyone walked from one hof to another. Many of the events took place in Isla, the largest of the three hofs. I remember returning at the end of the evening in the moonlight, some riding in the wagons, most of us on foot. Each of the hofs had a power plant that generated electricity, but they shut down at nine or ten in the evening. It was early to bed, early to rise at the Bruderhof.

When we arrived in Primavera, I was fourteen and puberty was hitting. The hard, physical work helped burn off some of my adolescent energy, but I experienced the same embarrassments that all boys go through at that age. The shorts we wore were skimpy and no good at hiding erections; the girls' dresses, despite being modest, revealed their budding figures. My friend Fritz's half-sister, Miriam Arnold, was a little older than me and probably never noticed me, but I noticed her. She was beautiful.

The Ibate Building Department. Left to right: Ed's friend Fritz Kleiner, Karl Keiderling, Ray, Gerald Dorell.

She later wrote a book about growing up in the Bruderhof and the painful experience of being expelled from the community as a young woman (*Cast Out in the World*, by Miriam Arnold Holmes, 1997).

Most of the work at the Bruderhof was split along conventional gender lines. My mother and the girls were assigned to the laundry, the kitchen, or child nurseries, and my dad went to work constructing houses. When we arrived, school was on break, and I joined Dad in the building department. Our first assignment was installing window and doorframes in a new two-family house going up near the library. With all the new houses being built, the sawmill had a hard time keeping up.

When school resumed, I joined the eighth-grade class in Ibaté. It took some time to make friends, and at first I spent much of my free time visiting the excellent community library, which served all three hofs. The families at the Bruderhof were large, and gradually I got to know other kids my age. One was Paul, the baker's son. He and I built a peanut-roasting furnace that produced a tasty product. I also enjoyed group horseback rides and swimming with the other kids in a farm pond or in a river, some distance away. On one of these outings, I slipped and split my chin on a makeshift diving board, sending me to the Bruderhof hospital.

Each of the hofs had its own school through eighth grade, attended by boys and girls. Youths who showed promise were sometimes sent away for more schooling, but most of the others went to work. I received German tutoring from Tante Käthe, the elderly sister-in-law of the Bruderhof's founder. Under her guidance, I memorized several classic works, such as Goethe's "Erlkönig," but I had a hard time keeping up in school. My teacher, Georg Barth, gave instruction in German. He did his best with me, but I struggled with the language. My best subject was physics, which middle-schoolers in the US don't normally study but had real practical value for the young people at the Bruderhof. I was fascinated with levers, pulleys, and mechanics in general. When Herr Barth demonstrated the concepts, I could more or less follow along. But in the other subjects, I couldn't keep up.

I was given an IQ test to see if I was a good candidate for high school; they decided I wasn't. They moved me down to seventh grade, and by August, I was out of school completely and working full-time with Dad in the building department.

Sabin Children at Tapiracuai River.
The Primavera vacation cabin was located on the river.

SEARCHING FOR LIFE'S PURPOSE

• • • ✦ • • •

The Bruderhof had lofty goals. Rather than waiting for some indefinite future, they were trying to build the kingdom of God on earth and live as brothers in the here and now, much like the early Christians as described in the book of Acts. They wanted to live apart from wider society but at the same time serve as a light for others. It's a hard thing to do.

Bruderhof philosophy held that everyone was equal, but in practice, some were more equal than others. My mother noticed that the family of the leaders seemed to do a little better than the other families, and that kind of thing bothered her. She was sensitive to hypocrisy. I suspect that she never really considered our move to the Bruderhof a permanent one; in October, four months after our arrival at Primavera, she and Mimi returned to the US. Dad and I gave up our two-room cottage in Ibaté and moved to Loma.

The Bruderhof was intended to be free of hierarchy, but in reality, the "Servants of the Word" led each of the hofs. In Ibaté, that role had been served by Hardy and Heine Arnold, sons of the founder. In Loma, however, our Servant of the Word was not a member of the Arnold family. Perhaps that was the reason the people there seemed more liberal and flexible in their thinking.

After a brief stay in a new hut, we moved into a building with residential rooms on one side and the hof's offices on the other. I kept a journal during this period, and the entries describe the rainy season, the books I read (a lot of science fiction), my German lessons, and my interaction with other young people of Loma. For work I was partnered with Fritz Kleiner in the wagoning department, the same boy I had worked with in the building department in Ibaté. Fritz, step-son of Hardy Arnold, was a jokester who frequently had a smile on his face, and he and I became friends. Another of my friends was his step-brother, Gabriel Arnold, a striking youth who was a tall, Nordic type with broad shoulders and blond hair. (Not long after I knew him, he moved to the US and died while playing in a high school basketball game, apparently asphyxiating on his own vomit). I also knew Christoph, the son of Heine Arnold. As an adult, he would take over leadership of the Bruderhof community, but I recall him as an awkward young teenager—not exactly a leader among boys.

In the wagoning department, Fritz and I worked under the supervision of Albert, a quiet bachelor from Swabia who wore a little felt hat and had terrible, discolored teeth. I still recall the awful smell of his cigarettes. Fritz knew much more about horses and wagons than I did, so he was the lead driver. The wagon was built of loose slats over a frame that allowed the front axle to move one way while the back axle tilted another, a perfect design for traveling over rutted roads. We sat on a board spanning the two sides of the wagon.

Each morning, we hitched up a couple of the small but tough native mustangs to a wagon and drove to the mandioca fields. Over the years, the Bruderhof used a slash-and-burn technique to clear the fertile ground where the forests stood, hauling the logs away for lumber and preparing the ground for planting. In fields littered with large, burnt pieces of logs, Paraguayan workers planted and harvested the root crop; the ash from the burning kept the ground fertile for a few seasons, and then the process would start over again in a new location. Delivering two at a time, Fritz and I transported a total of six long wooden boxes filled with the tubers to the community kitchen, where it was soaked overnight to remove the poison from its outer covering, then peeled and boiled, or occasionally fried, and served for lunch and dinner. The rest of our day was filled with other jobs, including hauling firewood to the kitchen and delivering kitchen refuse to the piggery, where the swineherd kept a cauldron of slop boiling.

The Bruderhof hogs weren't anything like what we have in the US. They were large, probably three hundred pounds or more, and bred to produce meat and, more importantly, the lard that was a key part of the Bruderhof diet. Once a week, Fritz and I were responsible for transporting a single hog from the piggery to the Bruderhof slaughterhouse. It was a big job. The swineherd or his helper roped a hog by its hind leg, and then it took four of us to slide it up a stout wooden plank into the wagon. We had to take care not to get kicked or bitten; they had big teeth. The hog was laid on its side and strapped down for the drive to the slaughterhouse, past the sawmill at the other end of the hof. The hog squealed the whole way there. It was horrible. At the slaughterhouse, the hog's throat was slit, and the blood spilled onto the cement floor and into gutters that ran out to the grassland. Vultures perched on the fence, waiting for offal.

The whole process of driving the terrified animal to its death was difficult for me and Fritz, just as it was for the crew of Paraguayans working in the slaughterhouse and the brother overseeing the operation. Every six months a different brother was brought in to take charge. It was thought that no one should have to do that job for longer than that.

That fall (spring in Primavera) we started making plans for my return to the US. Nancy, too, considered leaving. In Dad's journal, he wrote: "I guess she misses fun, zest, and the little adventures of places to go and things to do. I think that is a sad lack here. One can do things, but little immediately, spontaneously, or individually."

With November came the Paraguayan summer. There wasn't a big difference in the weather, except that now it was officially the rainy season, and the roads often turned to mud. Dad, Nancy, and I spent time in the community workshop making Christmas gifts: a table lamp, some ceramic items, and my personal project, three model sailboats.

On Christmas Eve, we walked with the rest of the community to the cow stalls to view a live manger scene. A girl named Lotte played Mary and held a real baby. Surrounding them were people dressed as shepherds and angels, including one with a six-foot wingspan. Live donkeys and sheep completed the tableau. Everyone walked home holding candles, and on the way, we stopped at Hardy's to exchange gifts and drink wine while sitting outside and listening to Handel's "Messiah" on a record player. The next couple of days were spent with leisurely walks and visiting other households.

CHAPTER SIX

A New Start

I had suffered from occasional bouts of "Paraguayan stomach," but now I had to drink a medicine that tasted like gasoline, the standard treatment for hookworm given to anyone before leaving the Bruderhof. My father recorded our weights in his journal: He was down from over 200 pounds to 169, and I weighed 121 pounds.

On a Thursday afternoon in January 1954, after saying my goodbyes, my dad and I climbed into a wagon and departed the Bruderhof. Dad would accompany me as far as Asunción before turning back. He still had thoughts about becoming a full member of the community and was not ready to come home. Nancy, too, had decided to stay at the Bruderhof for the time being.

Sometime after passing Itacurubí, our wagoner pulled off the road, and I cooked us a campfire dinner. That night we made a pallet with my poncho and some blankets on the clay tile floor of a little store. When morning broke, we made our way through a steady rain to Rosario, and from there we spent the night on a riverboat, arriving early the next morning in Asunción. A few days later, Dad saw me off at the airport for my flight to Rio de Janeiro.

I hadn't seen my mother in four months and was eager to reunite with her, but standing in the terminal next to my dad, I felt torn. He looked older than when we'd arrived in South America. The hard work in the building department and the plain food had whittled him down, leaving his face noticeably thinner. Would I see him again soon? Or would he make the Bruderhof his permanent home? I was willing to support whatever choice he made, but at that point, he didn't know what he wanted. It would take him another year to figure it out.

I boarded the plane with sixty-three dollars in my pocket (but not the scrap of paper with my mother's phone number in Denver, which Dad forgot to give me). In Rio de Janeiro, Reverend Legg, an American minister and friend of the Bruderhof, put me up for the night. I was lucky that he showed up to meet me; the letter from the brothers asking for his help had arrived just the day before.

The next day I flew to Miami, and the rest of the trip was mostly a long, boring bus ride to Denver, where Mother had moved after returning to the US. There was one unpleasant incident in the men's room of the bus station in Tennessee. A stranger, appearing from nowhere, asked me, "Hey, kid, want to earn some money?" I froze. A year or two earlier my dad had fumbled through an explanation of sex. Despite my patchy understanding, I knew enough to stay away from this guy. "No," I said and beat a hasty retreat.

After that the miles rolled by. Taking a long bus ride is like sitting in a stationary spot and watching the world speed past you. I was the fixed point, watching as one mile led to another. It had been a long time since I'd last been in the US, but all I felt was a yearning to be home—wherever that was now.

Without her phone number, I couldn't let Mother know exactly when I was arriving. On the evening before I was due in, she went back and forth to the main terminal multiple times to meet the busses; just after she finally went home and fell into bed exhausted and worried about me, my bus pulled in. I had no way of reaching her, so I did the only thing

I could: I sat down and waited. It was a joyful reunion when she arrived a few hours later.

For no special reason other than that it appealed to her, Mother had chosen Colorado to move to when she returned to the States. She had arrived in October, too late to find a teaching position. Now, in January, she was taking odd jobs, doing babysitting, and substitute teaching—anything to make ends meet. With Dad in Paraguay, she was the sole breadwinner.

I was happy to be back in the US, but I needed time to readjust to mainstream culture. I spent most Sundays at the Museum of Natural History in nearby City Park, sitting in the dark watching free showings of travelogues and nature films. The Bruderhof's attitude had seeped into me, and I was critical of all the wastefulness I saw, a product of the consumerism that contrasted sharply with my experience of the previous eight months. Still, I was happy to eat hamburgers and listen to pop music again.

At the Unitarian church in Denver, I made friends with two sisters, Joyce and Susie Kramer. Decades later, Joyce told me how homespun I looked in those early days after returning to the US. She recalled my mother telling her that she'd had enough of the Bruderhof when she had to knit stockings for our family out of string. "I liked you immediately," Joyce wrote not long ago. "I believe the experience of being at the Bruderhof was influential in shaping the young man I knew later in Boulder," she continued, referring to our college years in Boulder, Colorado. "You knew how to live on a shoe string, but more importantly your politics and respectful relationships to friends such as Susie and me demonstrated admirable strength of character."

In Denver that winter, I started school mid-year, my third and final experience as a ninth-grader. I was a little older than my classmates, but it was good to be back in school. I was placed in the top track at Morey Junior High but had to work hard to make Bs and Cs. I'd had some exposure to algebra and French, but starting halfway through the year was a challenge. I was in some tough classes.

We moved several times that winter, from an efficiency at 1415 Race Street, to an upstairs apartment at 1630 Ogden Street (with a roommate), to a finished attic at 692 N. Downing Street. None of them felt like home. We couldn't afford a car, but every new place Mother found was within walking distance of my school.

I had some problems with my teeth since returning from the Bruderhof, but with money so tight, Mother couldn't afford to pay a dentist. Instead, she worked out a deal with the Cody Dental Clinic: We cleaned their offices on Sundays, and they filled my cavities and did some work on her mouth. I also got a job at the local Safeway bagging groceries for eight hours on Saturdays. I was paid fifty-five cents an hour. Observing customers was a good object lesson in how I did not want to behave toward people. The way some of them acted toward the cashiers made me cringe. At the store we followed the dictum of "the customer is always right," and the beleaguered cashiers had no recourse when a customer treated them poorly. I felt sorry for them.

Mother was barely earning enough to keep us afloat, so when she was offered a position as a live-in helper for the Campbells, husband and wife physicians on the faculty of the University of Colorado Medical Center, it must have been a relief. We moved into the finished attic of their large Colonial on Downing Street, and Mother helped care for their children and the house.

Our attic wasn't equipped with a bathroom, so we shared the family's facility on the second floor. One day while I was washing up, Susie, the daughter, stopped in the open doorway. She had a lame leg and had been spoiled by her parents. "Ed," she said, "have you ever shaved?" I was fifteen and whisker-free.

I shook my head no.

"My dad's razor is right there. You should shave with it."

"I don't need to," I said. She was making me uncomfortable.

"Go on. He won't mind."

The longer she persisted, the more uneasy I felt. This is crazy, I thought. It seemed like the only way I could get rid of her was to do what she said. I reached for the razor.

Just as I was drawing the first swipe through the shaving cream on my chin, Susie spun around and called out to her father, "You don't mind if Ed uses your razor, right, Dad?"

Of course he did.

There were no dire consequences to my dumb move. The man was irritated and let me know it, but we weren't kicked out because of it. However, after living with people committed to a life based on Jesus' Sermon on the Mount, Susie taught me a valuable lesson about humanity: mean, not to say evil, people exist.

Living in a strange family's house was hard, but our options were limited. Mimi was at Antioch College in Ohio, scraping by on nothing. My mother, suffering from some disorientation upon being back in the States, had been told by Nancy that Mimi would need a party dress, so she and Mimi splurged on a dress plus a strapless bra. This despite the fact that Mimi had few other clothes and only one pair of socks. The dress was never worn and Mimi, with an extreme sense of economy, washed out her single pair of socks every night.

Meanwhile, the struggle between my parents was building. Mother had gone along with our move to the Bruderhof, but now she was pushing hard to get Dad and Nancy to come home. She'd done the same with me before I left the Bruderhof, sending letters that left me feeling guilty for not being at home with her. There was a game of tug-of-war going on, and I was in the middle. I wrote to Nancy and Dad in March: "I am kind of peeved with Mother because of her catty remarks and insinuations in her letters; it was quite childish."

Looking back on it, I don't think I minded Dad's absence. I sincerely wanted him to find the fulfillment he was looking for. But Mother had enlisted me as a foot soldier in her campaign to get him to come home, and I complied. Nancy made the decision to return, but Dad was still holding out, and I did my part to persuade him to come home. "I understand Mimi's reaction to the Bruderhof shortly after she got back," I wrote. "Issues are pretty one-sided there, you must admit. The things that seemed so important against America there are everyday things here and I hardly ever think of them… I still hope to visit the Bruderhof when I am older. Do as you think you should but come back first and see the other side. Your viewpoint will change and if it does not, you will become a better community member….Please don't take the same attitude to this letter as we did to Mother's. Try to see both sides….Well, write soon and let's hope that everything works out."

My Grandmother Sabin took a different approach. She wanted what was best for her son, and she reminded him that he was the only one who could decide that. In a letter she sent to him in Paraguay, she wrote, "My one thought now is that you have found contentment—peace of mind so to live your life to make the best use of it. You and you alone will have to decide that."

CHAPTER SEVEN

Evergreen

I found out about Evergreen through a cousin who had worked at the camp, Susie Sabin. The Episcopalian conference camp was in the mountains, twenty miles southwest of Denver, and hosted summer gatherings for religious educators, church musicians, youth groups, and others. I applied for a job and was the youngest of the eight teenagers hired to serve food, make beds, and do general maintenance. We were overseen by Kady Faulkner, the camp manager and treasurer. A no-nonsense art teacher at a private school in Wisconsin, Miss Faulkner smoked cigarettes in a holder and had once been a student of the famous German painter Hans Hofmann. Her work hung (and still does) on museum walls. During the school year, she taught at Kemper Hall, an Episcopal girls' school in Wisconsin where Gretchen Brant, one of the other teenage workers, was a student.

As staffers, we worked hard, but after spending six hours a day serving breakfast, lunch and dinner, we had free time to go climb the nearby mountains, walk into town, or wander around on our own. It was fun.

1954 staff of Evergreen Conference Camp. Back row, left to right: Richard Miller, Mrs. Olson, Miss Whitehead, Mrs. Douglas. Middle row: Roger Olson, Iris Vosholtz, Lee Burt, Gretchen Brant. Front row: Dick Kinney, Ed, Carol Cornwall, Kady Faulkner. Photo by Larry Lowe.

The camp's main building, Hart House, sat on a hill opposite Independence Mountain. The first floor housed the kitchen, dining room, and lounge and was wrapped with a deck (one of our jobs was to repaint it every other year). On the second floor were guest rooms; visitors also stayed in the cabins and two-story residences sprinkled across the grounds. Meeting House was a large, open hall with a stage that served as a classroom for some of the church music conferences. Bancroft, one of the cabins, had ping pong tables on its wide screened porch. I stayed with the boys in Nick's Cabin and Long House near Bancroft. The girls stayed in a cabin near Hart House across Bear Creek, the mountain stream that bisected the conference grounds.

Miss Faulkner wasn't sure what to do with me that first summer. Since I had no experience, she decided to have me fill in for the other kids on their days off. I swept and mopped the floors of the meeting house, picked up campers' trash, painted decks, moved beds, delivered blankets, and of course, served food. Meals were conducted cafeteria-style. Anything left over was put into bowls and placed on the tables for people to serve themselves. I had a good eye for portion sizes and kept us from running out of food before everyone was served, and that won me the approval of Mrs. Olson, the cook. In a later summer, I was promoted to assistant cook.

The camp was run by women, and one of its major benefactors was a woman. Anne Woodward Douglas was the widow of Canon Douglas, the man who donated the land and provided the funds to have the camp built. Mrs. Douglas had been secretary to the bishop of Colorado; she married the widowed Mr. Douglas when she was forty-five and he was seventy-three. After his death, she became the driving force that kept Evergreen Camp going through the years. I remember her as a dignified woman with gray hair, rimless glasses, and an ample bosom. Somehow we kids associated a painting of a headless male nude we found in storage with Mrs. Douglas, and it became a source of jokes.

There were only a few men associated with the camp. One was an Episcopal priest, Father Mordecai Marsh, a jowly fellow with a perpetual five o'clock shadow and a serious demeanor. I didn't often attend his services, but I remember him saying once of church rituals, "It's all symbolic." I understood him to mean that scripture was not meant to be taken literally. That stuck with me and is perhaps more meaningful to me today than when I heard it as a youth.

Larry Lowe was another male presence, and he became a big influence in my life. A

Self-portrait by Larry Lowe; his inscription, "Handsome, what! – that is 90 years ago"

former Princeton professor of modern languages, Larry had written a French-English dictionary as well as other scholarly works. He left academia and settled in Tucson, where he worked as a volunteer photographer at the Arizona State Museum. He was trim and neat, with a little moustache and an alpine hat topped with a feather, and he smoked cigarettes and spoke with the inflection of a man who'd spent lots of time in France. We thought he was terribly sophisticated and were flattered by his attention. He took us under his wing, especially the boys without fathers (with my dad in South America, I fell into this category). Larry talked to us about women and sex, peppered his conversations with swear words, and criticized American society and the boobs who ran it. His sensibilities were more European than American: He admired the Europeans' savoir faire and deplored what he viewed as crude and low in our own culture. He didn't have much faith in the common man. He may have been an elitist, but he was an elitist who talked to us like we were grown men.

"Ed has been getting some interesting letters from Dr. Larry Lowe, a bachelor who works at Evergreen in the summers. He seems to take quite an interest in the boy," Mother wrote to Dad. "He's another nonconformist and seems to be an interesting character. I mean to write and thank him for taking such a fatherly interest in Ed. I didn't care for some of the advice he gave him but—oh well—people don't often follow advice anyway."

Larry lived in the small caretaker's house with a darkroom in the back, and over the next few summers, he taught me how to shoot and develop photos. He also taught me some valuable life lessons. Here's one example. After I neglected to return a hammer I had borrowed from the tool shed, Larry didn't yell, "Return my tools!" Instead, he calmly explained, "Being a responsible adult means knowing that an object continues to exist even after you're done with it." The lesson was clear: being responsible means taking an extra step. It was an effective talk.

After the meals were over and we had washed the dishes, crumbed the tables, and swept the floors, we were free to do what we liked. One of the favorite activities among us boys was timing each other as we raced up to the top of Independence Mountain, about 740 feet above the camp. While one boy took off running, the others watched with binoculars from camp. It wasn't a sprint; to run up the mountain and then back down took an hour or more.

Carol Cornwall was a little older than me and a cheerleader at East High School in Denver, and we became a couple. With our small staff, she didn't have many boys to choose from. I relished my summer at

Ed rappelling down cliff; shot set up by Larry Lowe. Note the feather in his cap.

Evergreen. It came at a period in my life when I most needed it. My family was scattered and might stay that way; my dad was far away on his own quest; my mother was lonely, frustrated, and broke. Evergreen was a lifesaver.

CHAPTER EIGHT

Planting Roots

As Ed says, *what harm could it do for you to come to Woodcrest?* [the Bruderhof's new community in New York state]. *If you just stubbornly (it seems to me) hold out and stay in Paraguay, that doesn't leave any possibility of straightening things out. They will persuade you if they can for they are afraid to let you leave, maybe you're afraid too, but it seems to me that if your conviction were strong and deep enough, you wouldn't need to be. Do you agree?*
—from Betty's letter to Ray, January 22, 1955

My mother found a full-time position as a teacher in Lamar, Colorado, a town near the Kansas border, and we moved into an apartment on South First Street. Nancy was back with us, after having worked her way home as the captain's steward aboard a Swedish freighter. It was easy work, and she'd been invited to dine at the captain's table each night. In Lamar, she was taking community college classes in animal husbandry. Mimi was still at school at Antioch. Dad was the only family member left in Paraguay, and letters continued to fly back and forth. My mother wanted him home, but he still didn't know what he wanted. The longer he was gone, the less keenly I felt it. Mostly, I was happy to be in a real home. In Denver we had skipped from one place to another, but in Lamar there were no plans to pick up and move. It was a relief.

Returning from South America, we all had adjustments to make. My mother was warned by a well-meaning Presbyterian minister whose church we attended that we might be mistaken for communists. It was the mid-'50s, and Senator Joe McCarthy was whipping up fear about supposed communist sympathizers. Rumors alone were enough to put people out of work. When Nancy complained about the discrimination against Mexican-Americans in our area, it caused some heated arguments within her new group of friends.

When I look back on it, I see that our home life was disorganized, but it didn't strike me that way at the time. The same minister who cautioned my mother about communism had a great deal to say about theology in general, and in particular about the Bruderhof. His view was similar to my mother's. "He seemed to feel that it was definitely wrong to place the community as the end above all other things including marriage," she wrote to my dad. "He said he believed that Jesus would go to the Bruderhof but would not stay, but would get back into the thick of things again, even as he came into Jerusalem with the realization that he might be crucified. I believe he was right." By this time, I hadn't seen my father in a year; for my mother, it had been even longer.

There was talk about all of us reuniting at the Woodcrest in New York state, but Mother still pushed for my dad to join us in Lamar. "I agree to look around and see what the job situation is in New York and that's meeting you more than half way," she wrote to my father. "Lamar isn't so dear that I can't bear to leave it but Edward needs to 'belong' somewhere which he can't as long as he feels that it is temporary here. We're tired of being drifters, you can understand that."

All the bouncing around made me appreciate the stability of my new home, but it also gave me an outsider's perspective. I wanted to fit in and make a group of new friends at Lamar High School, but I also knew there was a wider world out there, a world I wanted to be part of. On weekends the teenage population of Lamar turned out in force, with cars full of kids cruising up and down Main Street. I thought there was something inherently silly about it but joined in. Cars snaked from one end of town to the other, with kids hanging out windows and talking to one another or pulling into the A&W for a root beer. The strip was a few miles long, with railroad tracks bisecting the "good" south side of Lamar from the less desirable north side. Sometimes, we had to wait at the tracks while the Santa Fe Chief and Super Chief stopped on the way between Chicago and Los Angeles. I wondered what the passengers sitting in the lighted train thought of us Lamar kids staring back at them. A feeling of disconnection ran through me; I was part of a group of kids whose horizons were no wider than the length of Main Street, but I knew there was more out there.

"Just think," I'd say as we sipped sodas at the bus station, "instead of spending this money on gas to cruise up and down the strip, we could drive to Mexico. We could get out and see the world." Friends just looked at me funny. They didn't see it that way.

As the new kid in town, I was still trying to figure out where I belonged in the dating hierarchy. I wasn't part of the crowd that dressed in the latest styles and danced well. Carol, the older girl I'd dated at Evergreen, wanted nothing to do with me now that she was back at East High School. At school, I asked a Hispanic girl to go out but she turned me down. Even though the Anglo-American and Mexican-American populations were thrown together, there was a definite social divide that few people crossed.

My school in Denver had been academically rigorous, but in Lamar I had an easy time with classes and made all A's. There was rarely a need to bring home any books because I got my homework done in study hall. Lamar offered some higher level math and science classes, and the kids who went off to college did pretty well. But the school didn't focus on preparing kids for college because most of them had no plans to go. Many were more interested in shop, business, and agriculture classes. I didn't mind the lack of challenge then, but it caught up to me when I went away to college.

I'd taken some French and studied German with Tante Käthe in Primavera, but in Lamar, Spanish was the only foreign language offered. It was taught by Mr. Bradley, who also taught English. He had lived in Chile for years and was well-educated, but he refused to let me share any stories in class about my time in South America. I'd already learned that I couldn't talk too much about it with peers without sounding arrogant and prompting a defensive reaction in them. Nobody came out and said

Dennis on his Steyr Puch motorcycle imported from Austria under the All State brand. Ed wanted one too but could not afford it as he, unlike Dennis, was saving for college.

it, but I imagined they were thinking something like, "Just because you've lived overseas and we haven't doesn't make us a bunch of yokels." I got that. What I didn't understand was Mr. Bradley's reaction. He and I had some common experience, and I felt I had something valuable to share, but clearly he didn't. Maybe I was just trying to come across as exotic to my new classmates—like how I sometimes wore my Paraguayan beret as a way to set myself apart. It probably made kids think I was odd rather than exotic. Whatever his motivation, Mr. Bradley wouldn't call on me in class.

Dennis Wacker was a fellow tenth-grader. He and his brothers were tired of people saying their last name with a short "a" sound, instead of with the German pronunciation they preferred: more like "Walker" than "Wacker." I knew enough German to get it right, and he appreciated it. He and I weren't much alike; he wasn't much of a reader until I introduced him to a few of my favorite war stories, and unlike me, he got terrible grades, but we became friends. He worked part-time as a printer's assistant and drove a small motorcycle that he bought at Sears. I didn't envy the job, but I did envy the motorcycle. He didn't need to save his wages for college for the simple reason that he wasn't planning to go.

The high school, which drew students from a wide area, had a WPA-built football stadium and track. I didn't know the first thing about the game, but Mother realized sports would be a good way for me to work my way into the school's social circles. She encouraged me to try out for football, and I made the C squad. It wasn't an impressive accomplishment; they didn't turn away anyone who went out for the teams.

Physically, football was the hardest thing I've ever done in my life. The coaches got us into shape with running, calisthenics, and scrimmages, all of it while wearing heavy, smelly equipment. By the end of practice, I was usually soaked in sweat, and after peeling off my sopping practice uniform, T shirt, pads, jock strap, and socks, a shower never felt better. The feeling of accomplishment after enduring one of our grueling practices was wonderful.

The next year I made the B squad and got some play time against the A squads of smaller schools, like Holly and Wiley. Since I was a fast runner, they initially put me on as running back, but I had no grit—I lacked the aggressive drive you need to run through the line. I did better when they switched me to linebacker. Tackling people and pushing them out of bounds appealed to my defensive nature.

I played two years before giving it up my senior year. I quit in order to earn money for college, but I still regret not going out for the team that last year. I'll never know if I would have made the A squad.

My only other sport was wrestling, and that was short-lived. But I did find that I enjoyed acting in the school plays. One year we produced *Our Miss Brooks*, based on a popular radio show made into a movie. For our junior carnival, I was bold enough to dress up as a female fortune-teller in a skirt, a head wrap, and big clip-on earrings.

With members of the Bruderhof beginning to settle at Woodcrest, there didn't seem to be any reason for Dad to remain in Paraguay. Even if he wanted to become a permanent member of the community, he could do that and live in the same country as the rest of us. However, my mother was still pushing for him to come home and help support the family. His responsibility, in her mind, was to get in the harness and pull his share of the financial weight. In my view, we were doing fine without him. And unlike Mother and Mimi, who were impatient and even outraged by some of the Bruderhof's practices, I held a sympathetic view of the community. If he wanted to join them and make it his permanent home, I was okay with that.

The tone in Mother's letters grew more urgent. Looking ahead to summer, she wrote, "It is only four months now so let's get hot on making plans...what do you say? If we put off getting together any longer, I'm afraid that 'spiritual divorce' is inevitable. As you said, we have been getting dangerously close to it and I feel it too." Nancy urged my father to consider a move to Gould Farm, a therapeutic community in Massachusetts where Dad's old friend and mentor Jim Adams and his wife had spent some time. Nancy wrote: "Over supper Jim Adams asked lots of questions about the Bruderhof...then went on to explain about Gould Farm. He and Mrs. Adams both seemed interested in getting you in that position...What do you think about it all? Do write us about your intentions or thoughts concerning it. I won't say anything because I don't want to stick my finger in it..."

A couple of weeks later came my dad's response: "Gould Farm is out...because although it is worthy, like a thousand similar good things, it has no idea of trying to change radically the 'normal' way of life." After a year and a half with the Bruderhof, he was convinced that an authentic life could only be experienced outside of mainstream society. It was exactly this notion that my mother rejected.

I still felt that if he wanted to stay in Paraguay, he should stay. But that wasn't the message that was coming across in my letters. I wrote, "You could just live with us for a visit before or after we all go to Woodcrest or something, but at any event it would not be too bad to visit us sometime, would it?"

After he received my letter, he wrote this in his diary: "Oh boy, mail today...Ed: 'For God's sake, people, please come back before making a decision.'" He didn't seem to notice the postscript I had written at the bottom of my letter. A message that seems a truer reflection of what I—and not my mother—thought at the time: "P.S. Actually I am not set against the Bruderhof at all but I think one should be sure."

By the time I returned to Evergreen in the summer after tenth grade, Dad was on a freighter headed to the States, working to cover the cost of his passage. In Colorado, my mother had a good job and a green, two-tone '41 Chevy (bought from O'Meara Ford, a dealership owned by a family she babysat for in Denver). Maybe it was the home and the car that convinced him to return to the land of pleasant living and consumption, although he was still considering a move to the Woodcrest

Bruderhof. When Mother drove to meet him at New York harbor, she didn't know whether their reunion would be temporary or permanent. He wrote in his journal: "I was hoping that Betty might meet me, but saw no one on dock. I went up to the bow and saw a tiny figure in a light summer dress, boy how nice to see her!"

They drove to Bronxville, New York, where Dad officiated the wedding ceremony for Mimi and Ben Drake, a boy she'd met at Antioch. Mimi left school not long afterward and moved to Fort Devens, Massachusetts, where Ben was stationed in the military. She later returned to college and earned a bachelor's degree.

Mother and Dad also visited the Woodcrest Bruderhof, where Nancy was staying before leaving for Albert Schweitzer College in Churwalden, Switzerland, a school suggested to her by Jim Adams. Albert Schweitzer was a Nobel laureate known for his humanitarian work, and the new school bore his name as well as his outlook. To earn money for tuition and travel, Nancy took a job waiting tables at Chef Karl's, an upscale restaurant in Lenox, Massachusetts. After my parents got her settled in Lenox, they continued their cross-country trip, stopping to visit family and friends on their way home. I would have to wait until the end of summer to see my dad.

This was the summer I learned how to neck. Except for exchanging a few kisses with Carol Cornwall the previous summer, I didn't have much experience with girls. Gretchen had told me her sister would be joining the staff, and she predicted that we would hit it off. She was right. Cynthia was pretty and quiet and had an interesting figure. She became my girlfriend for the next three summers.

The girls' and boys' cabins were on opposite sides of the creek, but it wasn't difficult to circumvent the watchful eye of Miss Faulkner when looking for a place to neck. Today when I smell mothballs, I'm transported back to the Meeting House and the "blanket box" where blankets were stored in the basement, a great place to neck (except for the smell moth balls).

Just like the previous year, we worked hard but had plenty of free time. We hiked up Independence and Bear Mountains and, on one memorable occasion, we slid down St. Mary's glacier. We hitched rides to Central City, a tourist destination about twenty miles from Evergreen, and ate pizza and listened to the honky-tonk music spilling out from the bars. We saw the Italian film *La Strada* at the theater and *Tosca* at the Central City Opera House. I borrowed Dennis' motorcycle, and with Cynthia sitting behind me and screaming the whole way, we drove down Bear Creek Canyon. She and I both blossomed at Evergreen. We were each other's first real love.

Cynthia Brant on a day trip to Mt. Evans

By late August, my parents had reached Colorado and were bumping their way up the mountain road to visit me. Later Kady, the camp manager, said I should have told her they were coming so she could have had a room ready for them, but I was too afraid she would charge us, so after spending the evening listening to records, Mother slept in the car and Dad bunked with me in the boys' cabin. It had been a year and a half since I'd seen him. "He looks so much like Frank [my dad's brother] and Nancy and Mimi," he wrote about me in his journal, "He is about 5'11" and is getting along fine at the conference camp...a great boy." Finally, Dad had made up his mind: He was home for good.

CHAPTER NINE

Finishing High School

Even though I hadn't been as anxious about it as my mother, I was glad that Dad was back with us. He was, too. In his journal, he wrote, "I pretty much enjoy the bourgeois life, coming home to a hot soak in the tub, a shave, and after supper sitting in the easy chair looking over the newspaper and library books, with Brahms' *First Symphony, Pictures at an Exhibition* or the beautiful *Pastoral Symphony* of Beethoven on the record player..." (the thirty-five-dollar record player I had ordered by mail from Lafayette Radio in New York). "I must say that our home life with Ed, where we have rabbit shooting and movies, or just being together for meals, is so much pleasanter than Bruderhof life."

I enjoyed spending time with him, too, and passed many afternoons in his workshop, working on projects. One especially memorable project: building a hydrogen gas generator to fill balloons. It exploded and spewed lye everywhere. I was soaking up all the things about him that, in a different way (some only revealed years later) showed up in me. Dad was staunchly anti-war and a supporter of the United Nations; I was a nascent peacenik. Yet we both loved traditional boy things: adventure stories, war stories, guns.

We went duck-hunting a time or two, but more often we shot rabbits, using the old single-shot rifle and a Winchester .22 single-shot we picked up for fifteen dollars. Dennis often accompanied us, bringing along his .22 and a 16-gauge shotgun, and we walked three abreast through the sagebrush, flushing out the jackrabbits. It took a surprising number of shots to hit them. You could tell where the shots landed by the bursts of dry dirt where the bullets hit. We missed more than we hit, and that was fine by me. They suffered a violent, agonizing death. It was hard to watch and in the end, it cured me of my interest in hunting.

Jobs were in short supply in Lamar, and it took Dad awhile to find one. He bounced around, doing manual arts therapy with the patients at the VA hospital in Ft. Lyons and working at Sutphin's Motor Works for $1 per hour. He even made an attempt to go back into the ministry, but it didn't work out. It wasn't until he started substitute teaching at the high school that he found his new career path. He signed up for correspondence classes at the state teachers college in Greeley and eventually earned his teaching certificate.

High school didn't get any more difficult my junior year, and I rarely came home with homework; there was so little of it that I managed to get it done during study hall. Mother and Dad worried that I wasn't being challenged and that I'd have a harder time in college (they were right). I had registered for social studies, Spanish, chemistry, English, and a math class that started with solid geometry and advanced to trigonometry, all "core" classes. But the school had a policy against students taking more than four core subjects at a time, and I was informed by the principal, Mr. Coffman, and the school counselor, Mrs. Applegate, that I had to drop one of them. It was crazy, especially since I was getting all As, but I had no choice. I dropped the math class. A few years later, when I was a junior at the University of Colorado, Mr. Coffman visited Boulder and met with some of us Lamar High School graduates. I told him his decision had hurt me, but he defended the policy, saying the school had to serve all kinds of students. I didn't take any math in college and have been a math ignoramus ever since.

Despite the school's lack of rigor, I had some fine teachers at Lamar. One in particular was Judy Hayes, my history and civics teacher. Whenever we had class discussions on the role of the US in the world, or the perceived threat of communism, or the meaning of democracy—all the issues that divided left from right—I voiced my liberal opinion. Ms. Hayes, like many people in Lamar, held conservative views regarding politics and society. She probably got tired of hearing me argue against her, but she never showed it. I argued for my beliefs so often, and with so many people, that my friend Dan inscribed my yearbook with, "To a good debater." When my dad was ready to do practice teaching, Ms. Hayes served as his student teaching supervisor.

I suspect one of the Lamar English teachers, Mrs. Weimer, was a closet liberal. She never had me as a student but maybe there was talk in the teachers' lounge about me. At any rate, she took notice of me and encouraged me to try out for school plays and to join the debate team. I learned about public speaking with the debate team, but it was painful. At a debate held in a nearby town, I forgot part of the State Department speech I was supposed to recite. No one would have known any different if I had just skipped over the parts I couldn't remember, but at the time I didn't know that. I just stood there frozen.

On another school trip, we stayed overnight in a hotel in Denver. The counselor who chaperoned us, Mr. Hartman, put all the boys in shared rooms except for me; he insisted I stay with him in his room. There was only one double bed and in the middle of the night I felt him creeping closer to my side. I froze, then rolled as close to the edge as possible. In the morning, he made an excuse about dreaming he was in bed with his wife. We were both embarrassed by the incident, and I never told anyone. Sexual abuse was not widely discussed in those days.

At the end of junior year football season, I got a job delivering telegrams by bicycle for Western Union. My pay was eighty-five cents an hour, and to make myself look official, I bought a blue cap from J.C. Penney and stuck a

From left: Doug Halbe, Ed, and Bill Kendall, waiting for homemade still to produce. Note the hot plate under the coffee can, the jar holding fermented fruit juice to be distilled, and the electric fan to blow on the wet paper towels to cool vapor coming out of the coffee can.

Western Union badge on it. Standing next to the telegraph operator when the typed message came through on long strands of tape, I could see that most of the messages to store owners were threats of legal action for unpaid bills. When I delivered them, the recipients and I both pretended I didn't know it was a dunning notice. There were frequent deliveries to the local haberdashery and to a florist. I found the whole thing embarrassing.

Even with school, football, and a job, I had lots of opportunity to have fun with friends. We went to midnight showings at the theater (one memorable showing: *War of the Worlds*), gazed at the stars at the University of Denver's Chamberlin Observatory, sailed the *Falcon*, my family's heirloom model sailboat, and drove up to Evergreen for weekend visits. On one or two occasions, Dennis and I took the DeLoach girls out on a double-date. We also went underground to explore the town's storm sewers, pinched watermelons, and once even stole some booze. That happened the night of the annual Cowboy Ball. Dennis and I waited outside as everyone went into the dance, then we swiped a fifth out of a pickup truck. We had been tipsy a few times on wine or beer, but this was our first time getting drunk. When we still hadn't come home at four in the morning, our parents got on the phone with each other. Dennis, who'd passed out in some weeds near the A&W, showed up first. Mother and Dad went out to look for me, then called the police station. Dennis's parents drove over to sit with my parents while they waited. It wasn't until the Wackers got into their car to go home that I woke up—in their backseat.

I was sick in bed the rest of the day, and my parents, understandably, were not sympathetic. Dennis and I were lucky to have survived alcohol poisoning. Since that day, heavy drinking has never appealed to me.

At the end of the school year I was back at Evergreen for the summer. Mimi and Ben visited, then took a canoe trip from Evergreen, intending to float down Bear Creek to the South Platte River and on to Greeley, where our parents had rented a place for the summer. When they reached the plains, the route was so clogged with irrigation dams

Hiking over Jones Pass with Mimi and her son, Jesse, on Ed's back

and other obstacles that they called me to come pick them up. They built a campfire on an island and sat down to wait. On the way there, I ran out of gas, and then, after walking a half-mile to the filling station and back, the car wouldn't start. By the time I reached them at midnight, they were asleep on the island, the fire gone cold.

Back in Lamar, I had dated a girl named Nona Cohen, but I was intimidated by the fact that she had gone out with a student at the junior college, and I never worked up the nerve to kiss her. At the same time, Cynthia and I were writing letters throughout the school year. At Evergreen, we picked up where we left off the summer before. One evening after our chores, we piled into a car and headed to Central City. I don't remember how we got the wine, just that everyone was feeling pretty good on the drive back to Evergreen. Cynthia and I crammed into the back seat with a few other kids, including Roger, the cook's son, but we didn't pay any attention to them. We were too busy necking.

The next day, Roger told his mother that I had been fondling Cynthia. He was right, I had (over her sweater, not under), but I couldn't understand why he felt the need to tell his mom. She passed it along to Kady, who came banging on the door of Long House Cottage, hollering to get in. There were two doors, and luckily she had chosen the one we locked before we started necking. Cynthia and I were on one bunk, Dennis and Carol Cazer on another.

"Why is it dark in there?" Kady yelled. "Let me in!"

She circled the cabin to open the other door, giving the girls time to rearrange themselves before bursting in. When she lectured us, she didn't tell us that what we were doing was wrong, but that it was "dangerous." It seemed like an odd thing to say.

Afterward, one of the other girls on staff told me Cynthia wanted to know if my actions in the car were just for fun or if it meant I was serious about her. That seemed odd, too. Putting it through my adolescent boy's reasoning, I decided the question was Cynthia's way of giving me permission to do it again. Maybe even under the sweater the next time?

Senior year came quickly. During nominations for class president, my friend, Dan Nickelson, moved to end nominations before any of the "in" crowd had a chance to get their names nominated. The list was short, and I won the election. (Dan had a sharp political sense and later in life would attain several high positions in government agencies).

My interest in photography grew, and with advice from Larry Lowe, I picked out a low-cost Japanese twin-lens reflex camera from Lafayette Radio. I took photos of everything, but my real interest was in capturing spontaneous moments around town. At home, I set up a darkroom, but without an enlarger, I could make contact prints only as large as the negative, two and a quarter inches square. For larger prints, I sent my negatives to Larry, who not only enlarged them, but also knew how to

This photo won honorable mention in a Kodak High School photography contest. Kodak notified the Lamar Daily News, which led the newspaper to offer Ed a part-time photography job. Larry Lowe enlarged the photo and darkened it to make it more dramatic.

make them more dramatic. One image I sent was of railroad tracks with a grain elevator in the distance. Larry enlarged it and darkened the clouds, and the photo won me an honorable mention and ten dollars in a Kodak high school photo contest. Kodak, being savvy with publicity, sent a copy to the *Lamar Daily News*, who not only printed the photo and a story about the award I won, but also hired me as a part-time photographer.

Working at the paper was wonderful. Suddenly I had access to a professional darkroom and photography equipment, including a press camera and an enlarger. During my first month on staff, I took a number of shots, including some of the local football games, but not many for the newspaper. That got me in trouble with the editor.

"We're spending lots of money on film and darkroom materials," he said. "Why aren't you giving us pictures we can use?"

"No one has asked me to take any photos," I answered.

From then on, I received requests from reporters for specific assignments. I bought a book on photography and studied it, and I experimented with shooting from different angles in different lighting conditions. Unfortunately, I didn't know not to light someone's face from below. My self-portrait for the school yearbook was ghoulish.

The newspaper also ran some writing I did with a friend, Dan Nicholson. Inspired by our trips to the Chamberlin Observatory, we ordered a telescope and began taking it out to his farm, where the night skies were clear and unpolluted by town lights. For a brief period, we wrote a column about stargazing for the newspaper, "Skies at Night."

An available light photo of Lamar Daily News press room

In Switzerland, Nancy met and married Bohdan "Dan" Chopyk. Dan was born in 1925 in Poland; as a teenager, he was arrested by the Germans and sent to work as a farm laborer in Germany. He became a displaced person (DP) after the war, managed to earn degrees in Germany and England, then landed at Albert Schweitzer College, where he met my sister.

It took months of wrangling before they could get Dan a visa to come to the US; finding money to make the trip was also a challenge. In December 1956, Nancy gave birth to their first child, Robin, in England. From there they made their way to the US and joined us in Lamar. That was the beginning of years of their living in close proximity to my parents.

Dan was a brilliant guy who knew multiple languages. Because of Sputnik and the space race with the Soviet Union, Russian teachers were in demand. He got a job as a high school teacher of German and Russian in Jefferson County, a suburb of Denver.

Both of my sisters' families grew rapidly during this period. After Robin, Nancy and Dan had three more children, Mimi Nadya, Bill, and Alex. Mimi and Ben had a son, Jesse, and then, after their divorce, Mimi had Jason with her second husband, Whitney.

In February 1957, I turned eighteen and started thinking about college. I was working part-time as a janitor alongside my parents at Likes Clinic, saving for tuition, but I still didn't know where I wanted to go. Mrs. DeLoach, the mother of the DeLoach twins, told me about Park College, which she had attended for a year. It was a small, liberal arts school near Kansas City where students worked twelve hours a week helping to run the college. It cost no more than our state university in Boulder, and I preferred a small school. They offered me a $300 scholarship.

Soon after my birthday, I received my draft notice. I wasn't sure what to do. Register like other eighteen-year-olds and hope for the best? Register as a conscientious objector? The Korean conflict had ended a few years earlier, and the worst of the Vietnam War lay years in the future, but the Cold War was in full force, and with it the threat of violence between the US and the Soviets. It was an uneasy time. In the end, I signed up as a conscientious objector. Between multiple student and teacher deferments, I never had to do the alternate service required of COs.

• • • ✦ • • •

Dad had a keen interest in rocks and mining. A Denver newspaper ran an article about a beryl miner near Salida named Harvey Moyer, and Dad arranged to visit him in early summer. He asked me to join him, and We met Harvey near the former Calumet Iron Mine, where Dad was interested in staking a claim. Most of the area had already been claimed up, but Harvey tipped us off about an expired claim a mile or so down Railroad Gulch from his cabin. We pitched a tent in the shrubs and shivered through a cold night, waking up to frost and some snow. On the second day, we drove down the gulch to where the road ended, then gathered our

Ray cooking on a Coleman stove on a camping trip near Salida, Colorado, 1957. Ray wanted to explore for beryl crystals. The peaks in the background are part of the Collegiate Range.

*1957 Evergreen staff, back row, left to right: Jo Carlo, Dee Bradshaw, Edie Young, Dennis, Carol Cazer (Dennis's girlfriend that summer) and Cynthia.
Front row: Skip Hankins, Mrs. Olson, Ed, Kady Faulkner and Chuck Hamlin.*

tools and started the long trek to the Split Rock claim. After hours of scrambling over rocks, we came to the end of the creek—and realized we had passed the spot without noticing it. The long slog back was especially tough on my dad; I was afraid it would give him a heart attack.

A few weeks later, Dad, Dan, and Al Wacker, Dennis' father, staked a claim a mile or so below Moyer's cabin; they named it the RayAlBo mine. They never found any beryllium, but for several years, the families enjoyed the shelter they built there. At 7,000 feet, it was a welcome getaway from the summer heat in Lamar.

After graduation, I returned to Evergreen. It would be my last summer working at the camp. Like the three previous years, it was a wonderful experience. My girlfriend Cynthia was there, and Dennis also joined the staff.

Cynthia came from a more traditional family than I did. Her father was an Episcopal priest, and her mother stayed home to take care of the family. Like her mother, Cynthia was the domestic sort. I was not. She was open to marriage, but I was heading to college in the fall, and who knew where life would lead me after that? One of the records we played in the meeting house was a 1930s oldie, "It's a Sin to Tell a Lie." The lyrics warned against being cruel to a girl who wanted more than a boy was ready to give. They struck a chord with me.

> *Be sure it's true when I say, 'I love you.'*
> *It's a sin to tell a lie.*
> *Millions of hearts have been broken*
> *Just because these words were spoken.*

I was in love with Cynthia, but I never told her. Happily, she and I remained in touch over the years.

CHAPTER TEN

Park College

n September 8, 1957, I arrived at the Lamar train station with my bags packed and ticket in hand. I would be riding the Santa Fe Chief to my new college on the same train with the same brightly lit windows I had watched as a high-schooler driving up and down Main Street. When we got to the station, we were told the train was running two hours late, so we turned around to wait at home. In the meantime, the train had made up time, so when my parents drove me back to the station, I had only a few moments to spare. I hopped on board with my bags, my guitar, and my record player.

Five hundred miles later, I was in Kansas City, Missouri. A station wagon was waiting to drive new arrivals up to Parkville, an old river town a few miles north, where Park College sat perched on a hill. By the time we arrived, I had my first crush. Cathy Holland was an incoming freshman from Texas—cute, friendly, and sweet. I didn't know if she was being nice and pleasant to me because she liked me, or if that's the way she was with everyone. I never worked up the nerve to find out.

Park had no fraternities or sororities, which was good in my view. Everyone on campus lived in dormitories. I shared a room with Art Rubin from western Massachusetts. It wasn't a party school. The atmosphere was serious and studious, and I enjoyed my classes, although my parents had been right: after an easy time in high school, I wasn't well prepared for the rigors of college. My mother was ready to work her fingers to the bone to send me to medical school, but I figured there were already plenty of doctors, lawyers, and engineers in the world. None of these professions would help me do what I wanted to do: help fix this crazy world. It was an idea reinforced by our time in the Bruderhof. I wanted to be part of that change.

Initially I planned to study psychology. Mother had taken some classes while I was in high school, and our talk at the dinner table made me think it was the route to go. But that changed when I learned about sociology, with its attempt to scientifically approach humanity's problems. I signed up for classes with the only sociology professor on campus, Professor Wayne Wheeler. I wasn't impressed with him as a teacher, but if I wanted to pursue the major, he was my only option. I also took German, one of several foreign languages offered. I remembered some German from Primavera, but in my second year I was exposed to a variety of German literature—poetry, plays, prose—in translation.

Park was unusual in that students had jobs on campus, a way for the school to subsidize tuition. That was important for me. My parents had received a $1,200 inheritance when Dad's Aunt Helen died, but even so, there wasn't much extra money for school. Also, the precedent had been set when Mother couldn't contribute much to Mimi's college education. At Park, students were mostly assigned to the kitchen, laundry, or janitorial department; I got the job of campus photographer.

I made some rookie mistakes. The worst was when the board of trustees gathered for their annual meeting. I'd been experimenting with a new technique using indirect lighting and had been pleased with the results, so I decided to try it out for their official picture. Instead of pointing the flash straight forward, I bounced it off the ceiling, thinking it would minimize any harsh lighting on their faces. To make matters worse, I took only one photo. Two rookie mistakes. The photo was so poorly exposed that the only way to salvage it was to send out the negative to be repaired. Even then the image was still too light.

In October of my freshman year, the Russians successfully launched Sputnik, the first man-made satellite to orbit the Earth. The news set off a panic, with Americans dreaming up terrifying scenarios of Soviet domination from the skies. We built more H-bombs; they followed suit. It was crazy and scary, and I needed to do something in response, so I started a chapter of the Student Peace Union. Two girls joined, a Quaker and a Native American. As peaceniks, we were outnumbered.

The chair of the political science department was a former Polish refugee. During the war, Dr. Jerzy Hauptmann had suffered at the hands of the Nazis and Russians alike, and as a consequence, he had become a firm believer in Realpolitik. He believed the Soviets were our greatest threat, and that we couldn't afford to hobble ourselves with ethical or moral standards when fighting them.

It was the kind of thinking that goes back to Machiavelli and the idea that the end justifies the means. In Machiavelli's *The Prince*, the title character can bring good to the people, but he can't expect not to dirty his hands in the process. I found this troublesome, because once you go down that road, you (or your country) lose your moral superiority and your hands get just as dirty as your opponent's. At the time, of course, our hands as Americans weren't as dirty as those of the Germans or the Soviets, whose governments were responsible for the deaths of millions.

Dr. Hauptmann had a following of students who agreed with his conservative views and who participated in the International Relations Club, which he moderated. The Student Peace Union members—all three of us—were encouraged to attend their meetings. We were his pet liberals, brought in for purposes of debate. Once or twice a month, we sat in a circle and talked about topics covered in their required reading, mostly

Newsweek articles about current events. Some of Dr. Hauptmann's students were ready to drop the bomb on the Soviet Union; I didn't think that was a sound plan for the future of the world. They argued for a greater show of force and a display of US dominance; we argued against it. I was intimidated at first because some of the students were seniors, but the atmosphere was informal and the discussions stimulating, and the debates were good training for all of us. Occasionally a smaller group of us would gather at the off-campus apartment of a young couple, Kent and Betsy Quinn, to continue our discussion. The Quinns' apartment was full of books, record albums, and candles with wax dripping down the sides of wine bottles. As a younger student, I was honored to be included.

My romantic life ground to a halt that first year at Park. Cynthia and I had parted ways, and as a freshman, my prospects on campus didn't look good. Also, it bothered me that I was still a virgin. Getting "unvirginized" is a big step for a young man. On Christmas break, I took a job selling advertisements for the *Lamar Daily News*, and one of the older staffers determined he should help me with my predicament. He took me to one of the two establishments that made up Lamar's tiny red-light district. An attractive, petite woman in a black velvet outfit interviewed me, then turned me away because I was too young or maybe too connected to the "respectable" class in Lamar. At any rate, I returned to school no more experienced than when I had left.

During my freshman year at Park, I took biology, English, German, psychology, P.E., and music. A Bruderhof teacher had told my dad I wasn't the brightest kid around (probably to justify ending my education with the eighth grade). When I finished my first year at Park with all A's, my parents were very pleased.

With Nancy expecting her second baby, my parents moved into the other half of a duplex Nancy and Dan were renting on the north side of town. My dad's days of searching for his vocation—and my parents' financial woes—were coming to an end. Dad finished the correspondence courses with Greeley, and both he and Mother were offered full-time teaching positions at a two-teacher school in Empire, Colorado, in the mountains about forty miles west of Denver.

The summer after freshman year, I took a job as a lifeguard at Troutdale-in-the-Pines, a hotel on the opposite side of Evergreen from the conference camp. My pay was room and board and several hundred dollars, more than I had earned at Evergreen. I was sad not to return to my old job, but I needed the money. Besides, it wouldn't have been the same at Evergreen without Cynthia. Dennis hadn't returned to the camp, either. He decided he wanted a college education after all and was busy earning money for junior college in Lamar.

It was a good summer, if not as life-changing as my time at Evergreen. I climbed Breckenridge Peak and planted a flag my parents could see, with binoculars, from Empire Elementary School. And I met a girl, Louise Holbert, who worked as a hired companion for a wealthy woman who summered near the hotel. Louise and I started going together, and near the end of summer, I invited her to come home with me for a family dinner. Without a car, our only option was to hitchhike to Empire, about thirty miles away. My parents weren't happy about me thumbing rides with a girl. I had done some hitchhiking, including one long trip from Kansas City to the Twin Cities, and only once did I encounter a man who wanted more than a passenger to share the ride (he gracefully accepted my refusal). It seemed like a perfectly safe way to travel, but they insisted I take their car to drive back to Troutdale-in-the-Pines. The next evening, Nancy called to say she was in labor. The only car in the family was parked outside my hotel room. It took a couple of hours for me to make it back, but we got Nancy to the hospital in time.

In my sophomore year at Park, I grew a beard, got a new girlfriend, and fell into a toxic rivalry with Jerry Plummer, my roommate. Jerry was the editor of the school newspaper, and I was the assistant editor. I'm not sure why I bothered with the paper at all; I didn't enjoy writing, and in the one editorial I contributed, I knew what I was trying to say but none of the readers did. Jerry and I were taking some of the same courses and were competitive with each other; the weaker and less confident I felt, the stronger he seemed to grow. It was a strange, unhealthy dynamic, and I finally moved out of our room and into a single room in an old dorm on the edge of campus.

My romantic entanglement that year was just as odd. I broke up with a freshman, Ann Mariner, to pursue another girl, Nancy McGrath. Nancy's campus job was to fold laundry, so she had her own key to the big laundry room, and we would sneak in there in the evening and make out on the long folding tables. Heavy necking in a warm room surrounded by the smell of clean laundry is a wonderful thing. Nancy was a senior and didn't want anyone to know about our relationship. She could be my girlfriend, but it had to remain secret.

It became clear that if I wanted to go into sociology, I would need to study someplace other than Park, which didn't have the courses I needed. My junior year, I transferred to the University of Colorado in Boulder. With in-state tuition, it was no more expensive than Park, and it had a large sociology department, just what I needed to prepare for graduate school.

That summer, my parents purchased the first house they ever owned, a roomy two-story in Idaho Springs, Colorado. The house was a ten- or fifteen-mile drive from Georgetown, the small town where they were now teaching, and it needed some repair work. Dennis rented a room from them for forty dollars a month and helped with the renovations. So did the rest of the family. One day while we were inside painting, Nancy started screaming for help. Dan had found an old paint can in the shed labeled "boiled linseed oil;" misunderstanding, he had put it on the stove to boil. It caught fire, and when he knocked it off the stove, the flames spread to the hallway. Dennis jumped to safety through a window, my dad ran outside with his pants on fire, and I scrambled down through a smoky attic hatch. No one was seriously hurt.

Dennis and I both got jobs that year with the Denver Water Board, working at Jones Pass on the Continental Divide west of Idaho Springs. The city water department had built a water diversion system to prevent water from flowing down the Western Slope. The idea was to keep the water in Colorado and not let it run to California. The water was diverted through a three-mile tunnel under the Continental Divide and into Clear Creek, and from there it ran naturally to Denver.

We lived in a cabin at the worksite on the Western Slope side of Jones Pass. My job was to cook for the crew of seven or eight, plus do light construction work between meals. Our schedule was two weeks on, one week off. Later in the season, when the snow had melted and the road over the Continental Divide was passable, we were able to drive a four-wheel-drive truck from one side to the other, but in the first few weeks, the only way to get to the worksite was through the tunnel. We drove up to the eastern side of the divide, loaded our supplies and groceries onto a three-wheeled Vespa, and rode three miles through the tunnel to the Western Slope worksite.

When I wasn't cooking meals or cleaning up afterwards, I helped with construction. We extended and maintained a series of dams among a latticework of creeks flowing down the western side of the divide. We built new dams and cleaned out silt from old dams. Pipes under dirt access roads directed water to a central collection site and then through the tunnel.

Another of our jobs was to shore up the main cabin with a concrete foundation. The supervisor, a man who dropped by every couple of weeks or so, instructed us to pour two feet of concrete under the perimeter walls—not an easy feat given that the rear of the cabin was built into a slope. Supporting the logs one section at a time, we dug down two feet, laid the forms, and poured the concrete. When we got to the rear of the cabin, the other guys and I modified the height to accommodate for the slope, but Dennis, a born perfectionist, wouldn't budge on his section: He had to get it to exactly two feet down. He labored over just one section while the rest of us slogged on, just wanting to finish the job. The guys weren't happy with him.

Dennis's attention to detail didn't survive the summer. Near the end of the season, we were stationed on the Eastern slope, an easy daily commute from Idaho Springs. The Water Board wanted to transport one of the large buildings to another site, and on our last day at work, Dennis and I were given the job of crawling under the metal building and attaching cheater bars to the wooden joists supporting the floor. They wanted to make sure the building wouldn't fall apart when they lifted it up to move it. The older crew members lounged around smoking and shooting the breeze, leaving the work to us. Denny and I resented it. Instead of driving the spikes into the joists, we banged around on the bottom of the building, making a lot of noise so the others would think we were doing the job. Then we crawled out and went home.

That was a bad move for Dennis. An inspection revealed what we had done—or rather, what we hadn't done—and a supervisor made the others do the job. As a cook I was a little harder to replace, but not Dennis. The next summer, I was the only one of us invited back to work.

In September, I gave Dennis a lift to Colorado State University, where he was enrolled in a civil engineering course. From Fort Collins, I made my way to Boulder and my new start as a student at the University of Colorado.

CHAPTER ELEVEN

University of Colorado

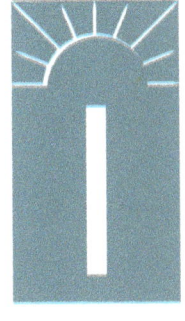I was eager to get a fresh start in Boulder. The school was much bigger than Park, and I was counting on it having a better sociology department. I didn't know anyone on campus, so I left it up to the school to find me a roommate. They gave me a small room in Aden Hall with a freshman from western Colorado.

My brother-in-law, Dan, was working on his master's degree at CU. News of the Cold War was hot then, and that, combined with my admiration for Dan, was probably the reason I signed up to take Russian. It wasn't one of my better decisions. My professor, a Latvian woman named Pachmus, was a stern, icy, Nordic type. Since I already had my foreign language requirement behind me at Park, I couldn't motivate myself to meet her high expectations. I was lucky to end up with a C.

Another class I took more than made up for it. It was a two-semester physical science course for non-science majors, taught by a PhD grad student. It covered a little of each of the physical sciences—everything from astronomy to physics, geology, and chemistry—but also included the history and philosophy of science. Most of my fellow students were there because it was a required course but I took it because I wanted to understand science, what it is and how it works. Over the course of the two semesters, I learned about what needs to be done in the social sciences—like sociology—in order to match the success of the physical and biological sciences. It made me see that we need to take the study of the behavior of humans and their societies away from philosophy, where people have been engaged in fruitless arguments for thousands of years, and subject it to the rigors of the scientific method. It's a tall order.

The secret, I learned, is that scientific concepts are neither right nor wrong, but instead useful or not useful. The useful ones can be applied to guide our thinking toward new paths and new discoveries, and with hard empirical evidence and math, we can progress. But we're hindered by the terms we use to describe human behavior. They're too mushy. They're replete with values, interpretations, and built-in assumptions. How can we hope to cure what ails society if, for example, one person labels someone a freedom fighter, and another labels him a terrorist? That's not science, that's politics. Take politics out of sociology and see what remains. Science is a process of agreement. If we can't agree on terms due to heavy value connotations, we can't build on each other's work.

At CU, I became friends with some students who shared my interest in social causes and joined the local chapter of the Young People's Socialist League (YPSL). Membership over the years had waxed and waned depending on political climate in the country, with a steep decline in the 1940's and '50s. But at the beginning of the 1960's YPSL was on the rebound and growing at a few progressive campuses.

I noticed that just like religious denominations, political groups tended to splinter into sub-groups with differing beliefs. Historically, the Left in the US was marked on the one side by those who called for a revolution. On the other side was the Norman Thomas and Michael Harrington brand of socialism, where reform rather than revolution was advocated.

Some of the YPSLs fell into the first camp. They were more radical than me, convinced that the way to change was through tearing down old institutions and building new ones from the ashes. I was more of a reformer. It seemed to me then (and still does today), that if you tear down a system, you have no way of knowing what will take its place. What if it turns out to be worse than the old system? What if you end up with a totalitarian state, something like what we saw in the Soviet Union? A better way, it seemed to me, was to allow for private enterprise, but also construct a social safety net for the people, especially those who can't compete in the marketplace. Don't start over. Fix the existing system.

The YPSL group was sponsored by Alex Garber, a sociology professor. As a whole, the members were earnest about making change in the world. Unfortunately, that wasn't the kind of crowd that attracted the cute sorority girls. I believed in the cause, but I also hoped to find a girlfriend.

Now that I was back in Colorado, it was easier to visit home. I didn't have a car, but Dennis had bought a '51 Nash with fold-down seats (good for making out with Carla, his future wife), and when his car was running (it often wasn't), he picked me up for quick trips to see my parents and to go skiing. If neither Dennis nor Dan were available to drive, I thumbed a ride. The roads in Colorado get icy fairly early in the season, and sometimes Dad, with mud hooks attached to the tires, would pick me up or take me back to school.

I spent Christmas break that year at home, and one of the events I attended was the holiday party at Mom and Dad's school. Normally Dad was the one to volunteer to dress in a Santa suit for the occasion, so it was funny to see the confused looks on their faces when they saw him in his usual clothes. Standing next to him was a younger and skinnier Santa—me.

After Christmas break, I moved out of Aden Hall and into the upper floor of a big rambling house on Pleasant Street with a couple of new housemates, Tim Kiovsky and Penn Kemble. Tim was a blond, bespectacled chemical engineering student from Colorado Springs, one of the few of our crowd who owned a car. Penn came from Worcester,

Massachusetts, and he had helped to start CU's YPSL chapter; he would go on to become the organization's national chairman, one step in what turned out to be a long career as an activist.

My girlfriend troubles continued, but I did get myself un-virginized. Beatrice Vogel was a little older than me and divorced, a stocky, ruddy, outdoorsy-type from Montana with a big friendly smile. She showed up at our YPSL parties and made it clear she liked me. After our big night, I sat in sociology class and couldn't stop smiling. Such was my delight at having overcome the burden of virginity.

An uncomfortable footnote to this story: Bea turned out to be rather possessive, and within a couple of months I eased myself out of our relationship. But apparently not before I borrowed a hiking backpack from her and then failed to return it. To my great embarrassment, she showed up at my parents' house in Idaho Springs asking for backpack. I didn't think I still had it; later, it surfaced when we were cleaning out the shed. I still regret handling the situation with her the way I did.

At the end of the semester, I went back to work for the Denver Water Board. I planned to take the following year off school and tour Europe. My mother wasn't happy about it. She thought I was setting myself up for a downward slide—that I'd end up a bum who never finished anything. But I was being strategic. I wanted to go to graduate school immediately after graduation and needed guidance and recommendations to do so, neither of which I yet had. Also, I was sick of school.

Jones Pass was much the same as it had been the year before, only now Dennis wasn't with me. I enjoyed the work but got tired of constantly being with the crew, so I took my bedding and an old oil lamp and moved into a ramshackle cabin in the woods a half-mile from the main cabin. Under a partially caved-in roof, I spent my evenings reading *War and Peace*; mornings I woke up early and climbed the hill to cook breakfast. Mother visited and stayed with me in the cabin. She had an adventurous spirit and didn't mind roughing it. Mimi and her son Jesse came from Ann Arbor, along with Mimi's boyfriend, Whitney. Like Ben,

Whitney was a graduate student in the English department at the University of Michigan, and they had started dating when Mimi's marriage to Ben fell apart. I had always admired the handsome and dashing Ben, but I recognized Whitney as a more solid type. I worked late into the summer, earning all I could before my big trip. By late September, I was ready to go.

Betty visiting Ed at his dilapidated cabin at Jones Pass, 1961

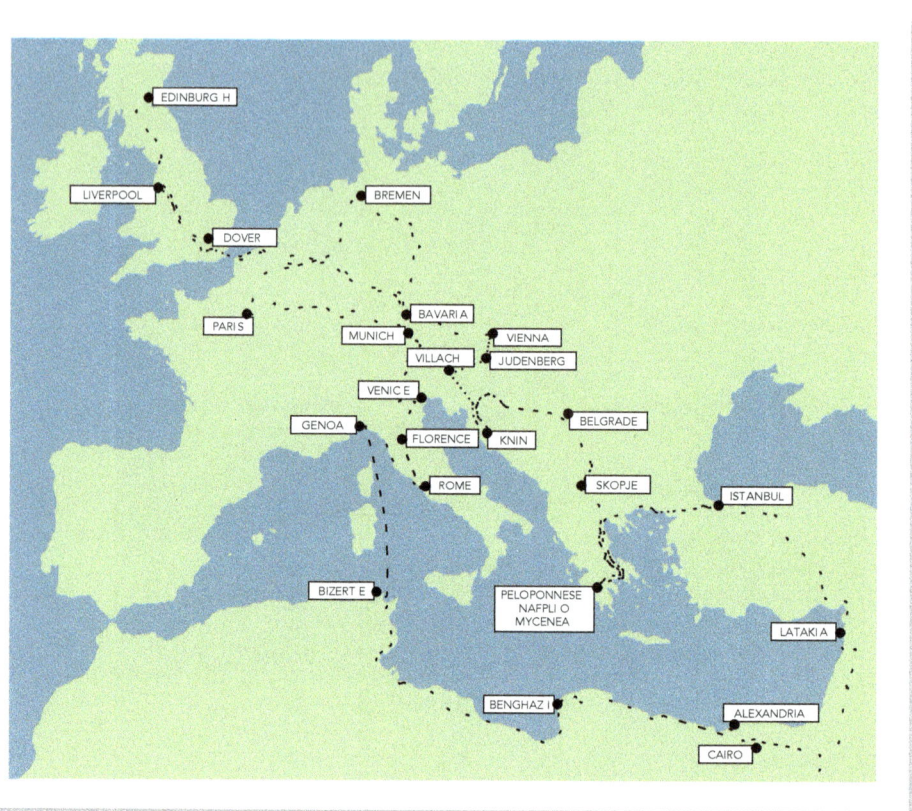

CHAPTER TWELVE

The Big Trip

Thanks to my job with the Denver Water Board, I had $700 in traveler's checks in my pocket when I climbed onto the midnight bus heading east out of Denver. My plan was to stop for a visit at Park College, then continue on to New York and from there to Europe.

Money tends to burn a hole in my pocket. At Park, a student, Bob Sprengnether, wanted to buy a Harley Davidson but was short a couple hundred dollars. He offered to let me ride the motorcycle while I was in town if I loaned him the money, and soon, my hard-earned savings had shrunk to $500. It was a dumb move; I still recall the berating I got from my parents when they found out. They complained that I was too trusting, and they were right. I didn't recoup the money until months after my return to the States.

After a few days, I left Park with a freshman girl and Sam Pendleton, one of Professor Hauptmann's gang. Sam had a new Volkswagen and a $7,500-a-year job with the Treasury Department in Washington, DC. In my mind, that was an impressive salary for someone just two years out of school. It gave me hope for a career in the social sciences. "That's with a degree in social science, not engineering, people," I wrote home, telling my parents about him. After a brief stop in St. Louis and another to drop off the freshman in Indianapolis, we reached Washington, DC.

The next morning, I took a bus to New York City and found cheap lodgings at the International Student Center, where I would stay while I hunted for passage on a ship to Europe. At the YPSL headquarters, I ran into Michael Harrington. At thirty-two, he was already a leader in the democratic socialist movement. An Irish Catholic from St. Louis, Harrington had spent a year or two living and working the soup kitchen at Dorothy Day's Catholic Worker house on the Lower East Side before moving to Greenwich Village. I met him just a few years before the publication of his book, *The Other America*, which helped galvanize Washington's "War on Poverty."

The International Union of Socialist Youth—the IUSY—was holding a conference in late October in Vienna, and when they learned I was headed that way, the people at the YPSL headquarters named me their official student representative. Now I had a destination—Vienna—and a deadline to get there. I spent the next few days looking for passage to Europe and, as usual, keeping my eyes open for women. One pretty Thai girl surprised me with her forward ways; I chalked it up to her having lived for several years in London.

Finally I heard about a ship line with low-cost fares that left from Boston. I made my way there by bus and knocked on the door of my Lamar friend Bill Kendall, a student at MIT. His roommates weren't too happy to have me camp out on their floor, but it saved me some money. The next morning, I walked in a gentle drizzle to Mendon, enjoying the famous New England autumn foliage along the way. I was hoping to see some of the people I'd known as a boy, but the only people I recognized were Putt Lowell and my old classmate Warren Goodnough, now the town barber.

Soon I was steaming across the ocean on the Furness Withy Line's *Newfoundland*, a 7,000-ton British mail ship that carried both freight and passengers. For a $300 round-trip ticket, I had a cabin with three roommates, two Australians and an American named Peter Nelson. On a three-day stop in Halifax, I spent the time reading and scheming to meet women—despite the fact that there were few eligible women on board. "I get tired of sitting in a circle and trying to put my two cents in," I complained about my poor odds in my journal. The style of travel didn't suit me, either. "The leisure and being waited upon is uncomfortable on the ship. I wish I were working my way over; however, observing a sailor's life on this ship, I see I wouldn't like it for long. Some of the romance of such a life as seen from Jones Pass is gone. I'm also impressed with *Of Human Bondage*—it makes me half believe in romantic love." Love and life's purpose: two preoccupations that burned brightly then, and still do today.

The socialist conference was starting on October 26, and I wanted to make sure I arrived in time. As soon as we landed in Liverpool, I caught a train to Vienna. The conference organizers had picked a good location. The socialist government was in sympathy with the IUSY, and planners were able to lay out a large spread with free food in a big, impressive hall. For students who weren't used to this kind of treatment, it was a welcome sight and, at the same time, it pricked at my conscience. "This is what a little power does to the most ascetic of us," I wrote in my journal. In the end, I was more impressed by the free wine and cigarettes than I was with the conference itself.

After the conference, I wasn't quite sure what to do with myself. My plan was to eventually make my way south; I had dreams of purchasing a Puch, the same kind of motorbike Dennis owned back home. In the US, Puchs were sold by Sears under the All State brand, but it was actually an Austrian bike. For now, though, the weather was too cold to go anywhere. I settled down in Vienna to wait for spring. I made several trips to a dental clinic for a toothache, and I read pocket books I purchased for fifty cents each, an affordable means of escape. I was homesick and out of sorts.

After sleeping under a tree one night (I missed the curfew at the youth hostel), I hung up flyers at the university, advertising for a roommate. Gys

Peeters was a Dutchman with a law degree who had come to Vienna to study tourism. He and I found a room in a rent-controlled apartment on *Sternwarte Straße* owned by a grand, aristocratic lady. She had her own room, Gys and I shared a second room, and the three of us shared a bathroom. Our shared kitchenette was handy for all the cheap meals we would be cooking over the next weeks.

From a letter I sent home:

October 31, 1960

We each pay $20 a month for this pleasant room and a shared bath and kitchen. This is a high price to pay but I got tired of looking and it might have been weeks before I could find a fair priced place since there is a housing shortage in Wien... This letter may precede one which I sent a week ago which carried, I now realize, insufficient postage and will, no doubt, go by ship. In it I must have sounded a little depressed and I was but I feel more chipper now. The main reason I feel better is that I've found a place to live. Last night was the first time I could really unpack my suitcases, put things away and not have to dig around in them.

I've been doing a lot of reading these days—pocket books and lending libraries here. It seems as though I've been doing this compulsively to fill up my time. It is an eerie feeling because it makes me ask, "What would I do if I didn't fill up my time with something?" Recently I saw some panthers at the local zoo pacing back and forth in their small cages. They went through exactly the same motions—several steps in one direction and then several steps back with a bang as their tail hit the wall. This was activity only to avoid sitting or standing and dumbly looking out. We should be thankful that we believe in education and self-improvement since this keeps a person's time full; for example, by reading "improving" books.

Our landlady next door (an educated woman) who must be a widow doesn't seem to have the value of self-improvement to fill her time. I hear her often shuffling cards for her games of solitaire. I'm not talking about boredom which is really yawning in the face of perhaps varied endeavors but rather fear of inactivity. Life has been defined as the struggle to make ends meet or action for tomorrow. I wonder if a man could sit and do nothing without going nuts?

The landlady frowned on our being home during the day, so to occupy myself I sat in on a German class at the university or took refuge from the cold at the American Embassy, where I continued to devour English-language books. My mother wrote to tell me she was worried about my lack of direction. I was questioning myself, too, wondering what I was doing so far from family and school, but I still thought her comments were unfair. "I'm about as 'flighty,' Mother, as a New England farmer," I wrote. "I methodically planned for this trip last year.... I plan to return to C.U. next fall and go to graduate school the following year. I'm not trying to escape anything."

There was nothing akin to sociology at the university in Vienna; the field of study appeared to be something specific to America, something I hadn't expected. It dawned on me that if I wanted to be a sociologist, I wouldn't have the choice of living abroad. In my present state of mind, that didn't bother me much. Living in one place or another struck me as all the same.

Gys and I ate most of our meals in the room, and they usually consisted of bread and cheese with sausages we cooked on the little stove. Another frequent meal was boiled eggs with toast and marmalade, and occasionally I treated myself with a trip to the butcher shop for 300 grams of *Rinderhackfleisch* (ground beef), which I cooked into a hamburger and ate with beans. I made a point of finding out what the average day wages were for the working man in Austria (and for every country I subsequently visited). The cost of food was the same as back home, but the average laborer earned far less than in the States, so I couldn't see how they made it work. It even cost money to sit on a park bench in Vienna, not that I wanted to sit outside in the cold. The only time I felt warm was in bed, at the movies, or at the library.

I kept up a steady correspondence with my family. Mother and Dad sent some money from Aunt Helen's inheritance, a generous act since they still weren't financially free themselves. (Dad said Aunt Helen's money allowed them to "get out of 'deeper in debt.'") I took a couple of odd jobs—digging at a ski area for forty cents an hour, tutoring a boy in English for eighty cents an hour—but mostly I just continued to read, study German, and save for my motorbike trip. Dating wasn't an option and wouldn't have been even if I had known more girls. It was too expensive. Also, without a car, it would have meant walking around in the cold. I conserved money and body heat by staying in.

I wasn't having any more fun in Vienna than I'd had back home, but each time I tried to plan my travels, I ran into obstacles. Train tickets were an expense I couldn't afford. I wanted to go by motorbike, but I had loaned my driver's license to an underage friend at Jones Pass and never got it back, a stupid mistake. Without a license, I wasn't allowed to drive anything bigger than a moped.

My parents got everything straightened out. They contacted my friend, got the license, and sent it to Vienna. At a government office, I was issued an Austrian license, and in December, I paid $120 for a used, two-stroke, 175 cc Puch. It was a nice bike, about the same power as a motor scooter but shaped like a motorcycle. Later, when I had problems crossing borders, the motorbike would become a liability, but for the moment it felt like my means of escape. I was eager to leave Vienna and the cold winter behind.

I made arrangements with a friend to drop off one suitcase in England, then packed everything else into a leather suitcase (from Paraguay) and strapped it onto the motorbike's rear rack, along with my sleeping bag and a large-scale map showing multiple countries.

My first wipeout happened before I got out of town. I slid on the wet cobblestones and toppled over. The only damage was a skinned knee and a dented bumper, but it put the fear of God in me. I bought a second-hand aluminum helmet with earflaps, protection against crashes and the cold. A major snowstorm blew across the city the day before I was scheduled to leave, and I prayed it wouldn't turn into a blizzard. It didn't. On December 14, 1960, I was on my way.

My goal was to travel south in search of sunshine and warmer weather. I planned to ride through Yugoslavia to Greece, and from there to Turkey. Europe's economy hadn't recovered fully from the war, but Vienna had been more expensive than I expected, and I was holding tight to my American dollars, hoping they'd go farther as I headed south and east. Once outside of Vienna, I stopped every five miles to warm up, and the motorbike slid out from under me three more times before I made it over a low pass into Judenberg, 125 miles from Vienna. The next morning I took a train to Villach, a small Austrian city near the border of Italy and Yugoslavia. It cost two dollars in freight to ship the motorbike, and it wouldn't arrive in Villach until two days after I did, but it was worth it. I didn't want another freezing day of fighting the icy roads.

Based on its location, I expected warmer weather and less snow on the roads once I left Villach. I checked my map and saw a major highway that ran all the way down the west coast of Yugoslavia. A couple of days later I was on the coastal highway, happy to be in the sunshine. This is what I had come to Europe for: to travel and explore, to see new places and meet new people. The scenery was beautiful. I rode a hundred miles down the Italian coast, with an overnight stop in Trieste, before I crossed into Yugoslavia. I was impressed by the country's natural beauty but dismayed by the poverty. There were few cars on the road, and I didn't see many restaurants or stores. Being accustomed to capitalism, I was struck by the absence of shop signs. I could usually find someone who spoke German, but when I did, they assumed I was German and that changed their mood; the locals weren't fond of their former occupiers. Sometimes I tried to make myself understood in Russian but never in English. Nobody spoke it.

I spent a night in a fishing village and then continued south on the coastal highway. I was enjoying the passing scenery and looking forward to the coming warmer temperatures awaiting me in Greece and beyond.

My doubts about the Puch disappeared along with the snow. Yes, it had been tough going in Austria, but now I'd be seeing new countries the way I had intended, zipping along (if thirty-five miles per hour can be called zipping) the roads and stopping in whichever towns and villages looked interesting.

I'd spent hours looking at the map, planning my route. First, I would take the coastal highway down the length of Yugoslavia, jog around Albania, pass through Macedonia, and arrive in Greece, where I would stop to explore for a week or so. Then I'd be off to Turkey, Syria, and Egypt. My mother's doubts about my future and my ability to plan still rankled; I felt capable of steering my course. "Do not worry, Mother," I wrote, "I know only too well that one must be careful on a motorbike and I will be. Also I'll check with embassies and ask them if it's O.K. for an American to travel in aforementioned countries." Egypt still seemed a far way off, but I had a vague notion of traveling across the top of North Africa and catching a boat from Tunis to Sicily. The southern latitude was appealing.

And then, without warning, just 125 miles south of Trieste, the highway came to an abrupt end. I pulled out my map. The line marking the highway continued, just as I'd seen before, but what I hadn't noticed was that it wasn't built yet (it was constructed shortly after my stay in Europe).

I spent several hours looking for an alternate road south, but it was useless. There was nothing along the coast. In the town of Benkovac, I approached a young woman for directions, and she offered to put me up for the night. After eating my first home-cooked meal in months, I sat at her kitchen table and wrote a letter home. "Finding my way through the country this afternoon on muddy dirt roads looking for a real road, I was reminded of Paraguay very much. I will be glad to get out of this hellish 'end of the earth' feeling. The motor bike is still running O.K. for which I am thankful—if it broke down I would be in real trouble." (It would later break down, more than once.) "I wished the last two frustrating days to be home again taking life easy but I guess I will see it through." I also wrote to Marietta, an English girl I knew from Vienna. We had planned to meet in Athens, but with this detour, I would be delayed.

The next morning I left for Knin, about forty miles inland on a muddy, chuck-holed dirt road. At the train station, I bought tickets to Belgrade, one for me and one for the Puch. It was a big expense, especially since I had to pay at the official exchange rate. On the black market, I could have gotten double the amount of dinars. Outside the station, a group of girls in traditional dress broke out into a spontaneous dance; I think they were just trying to get warm.

From a letter home

December 21, 1960

Just a note to tell you that I made it back to civilization, that is, Belgrade. I got here by train this morning after an all night ride. I will spend a day and a night here but not longer since an English girl from Vienna may be waiting for me in Athens. She may have taken a train down (much smarter) and we were going to motor bike around Greece for a few days.

Tomorrow I get back on the train and go down to Skopje (motor bike in the baggage car) and then start again on a paved road all the way to Greece, and not just half way as the coast road turned out to be. Bad roads in this or that country is a common topic of conversation in youth hostels. Now I understand why. I was too used to an industrialized country like America or Austria and so was caught by surprise. Let me plug the American 'broad but mediocre' educational system after seeing a lot of the 'true' peasant of Yugoslavia—or any underdeveloped country. The American educational system at least gives a veneer of civilization...."

CHAPTER THIRTEEN

On the Move

After a night in a Belgrade youth hostel, I caught a train to Skopje, Macedonia. I was in a hurry to get to Athens, where my parents were sending money from an emergency fund I'd left with them. After the unexpected expense of the train tickets, I was low on funds.

The road from Skopje was good, and the two-day motorbike ride to Athens was uneventful. On the border of Greece, I exchanged money, walked into a delicatessen, and splurged on a pastry. I was back in the free market again, but I didn't have the hang of Greek money yet. I held out my hand and let the cashier take what she needed.

I spent the last few hours driving in the rain, with snow-capped Mt. Olympus dominating the horizon in front of me and the Aegean beside me. It was Christmas Eve when I pulled into the city; bad timing, because it'd be two days before the American Express office opened. Wet and tired, I met Marietta, the English girl from Vienna, at a hostel full of student travelers.

I spent the next couple of weeks exploring, timing my visits to the famous sites to coincide with their free-admission days. The days were warm and the sky a deep, cloudless blue. Compared to the Soviet bloc countries, Greece was full of visitors of all nationalities. I was invited to join a guy with a VW on a driving tour of the eastern Peloponnese, and on New Year's Eve, we spent a mild, moonlit night in Nafplio, climbing to a castle and rowing a boat to a harbor fort. We also visited Mycenae, where we maneuvered our way through small tunnels, searching for secret passageways in the ruins of the citadel. That day was rainy and foggy, and the nearly deserted ruins were more enchanting than anything else I'd yet seen in Greece.

After spending a couple weeks with kids from the youth hostels, I got tired of all their enthusiasm and the endless talk about where to find bargains on food and travel. "The last two weeks I've noticed that youth hostelers (including myself) do favors for other people for the purpose of getting something out of it," I wrote in my journal. "When a favor is not repaid, you can hardly reproach anyone. It is much better to refuse a favor when it is asked if you have another purpose in mind. In this view I am wondering if I will take this Sally [Sally Collingberg, a Chicagoan I met at the hostel] for an excursion tomorrow." "Freedom," I mused, "lies in being honest with other people in what you are willing to do."

The Greek people were wonderful, very outgoing and friendly. One day when I was in a little town enjoying a cheap meal, a local version of bean soup, a man at a nearby table started talking to me in broken English. He was a farmer, or maybe a shepherd, and it took me a few minutes to decipher what he was saying. In exchange for a good number of sheep, he offered to let me marry his daughter and bring her back to America. I politely turned him down.

After ten days at the youth hostel, I escaped to the Hotel Colonial. It cost an additional three drachmas per night, but it gave me my own space. I replaced the dim light with a 100-watt bulb and read books I checked out at the American Information Service Library, including *Exodus*, by Leon Uris, to prime me for my upcoming travel to the Middle East. I also found an American sociological journal. When I got tired of my room, I sat and read in the America House. In between, I stopped by the American Express Office—repeatedly—to see if my fifty dollars had arrived from home yet. Until it did, I could only drool over the pastries in the shop windows, extravagances I couldn't afford. Instead, I made do with tea and toast prepared over a can of Sterno. "I'll have to cut out buying extraneous stuff these next few days until money gets here," I wrote in my journal. "I'm not anxious to get on the road again but hope for good weather when I do go."

My plan was to motorbike to Istanbul and buy a half-price student train ticket to a stop just shy of the Syrian border. But a few miles past Thebes, the engine on the Puch froze up. I found a mechanic, but he didn't have the parts needed to repair it, so I hitchhiked back to Athens and bought a connecting rod. While I waited for the repairs, I met an old Greek man, and he invited me to stay with him while waiting for the motorcycle repair, which I did. He told me he had immigrated to America as a younger man, but once he retired, he returned to Greece, where his Social Security payments went farther. Now he was lonely; all his friends and family were long dead. He asked me to send him a postcard from my travels. To this day, I regret that I never did.

I hadn't planned on staying in Istanbul, but after paying the mechanic seventeen dollars, I didn't have enough money to make it all the way to Cairo. I wrote home and asked my parents to forward money to the American Express in Istanbul. With the last few remaining dollars in my pocket, I pointed the motorbike north and headed for Turkey.

From a letter home:

January 24, 1960

The money arrived late yesterday at American Express and I picked it up this morning. Thank you so much for your prompt reply. I still had 7 bucks so I was getting along O.K. I'm staying here in Istanbul in a Turkish version of the YMCA. It's comfortable, has a warm reading room and hot water, though we must sleep in an icy dormitory. I have been here since Friday night when I got in on the train from 150 kilometers this side of Salonica in Greece, where it just became too damn cold to ride the bike....

I had gotten sick of other student travelers, but after I left Greece, the cold hours between sunset and bedtime had been hard to fill. When I did manage conversations with the locals, I heard the same questions over and over: How much did my shoes cost? My watch? My motorbike? "The result is always the same," I wrote in my journal. "The seeming unfairness that the man should work all day and still never be able to buy a radio, etc."

In Istanbul, I met up with Sharon Kalass, a girl from Park College. She had taken a government job in the city and was living with two American roommates in a big apartment overlooking the Bosphorus. I spent a couple of enjoyable evenings with them, watching the ferryboats, freighters, and Russian tankers through their big picture window. I also befriended a South African architecture student. Contrary to my previous opinion, it felt good to be with other students, sitting around in whichever hostel or hotel room was heated, sharing cheap meals of bread, cheese, and *Wurst* as we talked about our travels.

After my money arrived, I left Istanbul by train to southeast Turkey. I began traveling by motorbike in Adana and then on to Iskenderun, the first place in Turkey that was warm and semi-tropical. There weren't many hostelers, and I felt lonely during the few days I was there. The Turks were eager to try out their English on me, and it began to annoy me; even worse was the "pestering sort of helpfulness" (as I complained in my journal) which left me feeling like they wanted something in return. It was a common complaint among us student travelers. A chance conversation with a Turk fluent in English helped my attitude, but it left me so homesick and hungry for conversation that I started hanging around the reading room of the US consulate just to see some Americans. "I seem to have very little desire to get away from Americans or other tourists 'to really see how the real people or folk live,'" I complained in my journal. "Maybe I know too well already how Syrians live."

By the time I got to Antioch, I was so cash-poor that I was living on bread and margarine and sleeping in the police station. I needed to get to Syria to cash a traveler's check, but the Syrian officials wouldn't let me cross with my motorbike unless I had a "trip tik." What the heck was a trip tik? I had never heard of one. I learned it was an insurance policy issued by an automobile club to guarantee I wouldn't sell the motorbike in country (without paying an import duty). An older German-speaking man camped out at the border let me share his tent while I tried to get the issue straightened out. We communicated in German, and he didn't believe I was American. I was flattered.

There was no other option but to leave the motorbike behind and hitchhike to Aleppo to get the trip tik. At the automobile club in Aleppo, I pleaded my poor student status and they knocked down the price from eighteen to fourteen dollars, on condition that I would mail it back to them when I no longer needed it in Europe (I later sent it). I returned for my bike, got a room at a little hotel in Idlib, cashed a traveler's check, and bought some food. It was a little easier to take a philosophical view of the recent frustrations on a full stomach. "I stop and sit down on the sunny side of someone's stucco wall, smoke a cigarette, and relax," I wrote home. "One thing I reflect on is the role officials play in underdeveloped countries...."

All of my free time brought up questions on how to spend it; it struck me as a problem unique to the modern era. Earlier generations were too busy surviving to face the void of leisure time. "We need to fill up the time until we die but the question is, with what?" I asked in my journal, thinking about the caged panther back at the zoo in Vienna, pacing endlessly back and forth. The sociologist in me wondered about this new phenomenon. "This is a new problem in the history of the human race."

I was impressed with the narrow Roman stone road that ran parallel to the modern highway in places. It snaked up and down barren hillsides as I drove along beside it. The stones were raised slightly above ground since the latter had eroded away and the closely fitted stones had not. Syria seemed more Islamic or traditional than Turkey. I was struck by the women in black veils and baggy pants bound at the ankle ("They remind me of you, Mother, in last year's baggy slacks"), and the men in their red fezzes or long scarves wound around their head. Three years earlier, Syria and Egypt had combined to form the United Arab Republic, and pictures of Nasser hung everywhere. It wouldn't last, but for the time being it meant bargain ticket prices for travel between the two countries.

When I arrived in Latakia, a port city in Syria, I met a student who offered to show me around. Afterward, I discovered he had lifted my good sport shirt. "It makes me wary of people, especially the long-lost friend types who happen to know some English," I wrote. "It's maddening."

I was anxious to get to Cairo, where I could pick up mail, visit the American library, and soak up the warm weather. In my mind, Egypt somehow represented home. "Tomorrow morning (Allah be Praised)," I wrote, "I will get to Latakia, my goal for the last four days, and spend a couple of quiet days waiting for the ship to Egypt. It is mostly this damned bike which makes things so complicated. We're still having cold weather around here. I guess it will be Egypt before it is really warm."

In my last days in Latakia I made several visits to the SS *Buckeye State*, an American freighter on a foreign aid mission to deliver surplus American wheat. I wandered aboard looking for English-language magazines, but what I really wanted was the chance to talk to some Americans. It worked. The crew had been confined to the ship during the seventeen days they were docked in Latakia and were happy to see a fresh face. I was invited to join them for dinner, a ritzy affair with waiters serving steak, but after listening to them shoot the bull for a few hours, the romance of the seaman's life wore thin. The job provided good pay and good food, but overall it seemed like a boring life. To stir up some trouble, one of the sailors told the locals bagging and unloading the wheat that the franks they were eating—courtesy of the crew—contained pork. It was a mean thing to do and it caused a commotion.

The next day I was on board the *Myrs*, headed for Alexandria. A storm blew up and what was supposed to be a day and a half voyage turned into three days on board the rocking, heaving boat. My deck-class ticket included a bed in the hold, with bunks stacked three high, but I spent most of my time in the second-class lounge to escape the unpleasant below-decks. I was one of few passengers who didn't get seasick. When people weren't puking, they were competing to see who could out-spit each other. The floors were slimy.

After a couple of days in Alexandria, I drove southeast through the desert. The sight of the pyramids slowly looming into view in the desert was thrilling. So was passing from desert into the Nile Valley. I was relieved to reach Cairo, where I expected letters and money at the American Express office. The letters showed up, but the money did not. My disappointment showed when I wrote home: "Evidently I did not make it clear in my last Athens letter or in my Istanbul letter that you should send $50 to me in Cairo. Perhaps you thought the $50 sent to Istanbul would substitute for the money here? In any case I hope that you received my letter from Idlib in Syria and that I hinted in that letter that I would need some money in Cairo." I convinced the American Consulate to loan me some money, and back home the family scrambled to send cash. Things were tight with them, too. My sister's husband, Dan, withdrew eighty-five dollars but sent it through the embassy rather than American Express, causing a delay. "Letter from Ed: 'Please send money.' Pop, groan, shudder, trouble!" my dad wrote in his journal. "All very low on money! Cashed a post-dated check today at Gamble's store to tide us over."

Egypt surprised me. It wasn't at all the "land of pharaohs" that I'd read about. In Cairo very little ancient history was in evidence. Despite the pyramids in the distance, this was a city for the living, not the dead. It was also the first country I'd been in where Americans weren't popular. The Egyptians didn't like the way African Americans were treated in the US; they were upset that we had refused to help Egypt build the dam at Aswan; and they were enraged by the US support of Col. Mobuto in the Congo.

In Cairo, I found myself standing at the edge of a crowd of protesters. Just a month earlier, Mobuto's rival, Lumumba, had been tortured and executed. I was careful not to identify myself as an American. The crowd surged toward the American embassy, where they broke windows and set fire to a couple of embassy cars. Then they made their way to the nearby Belgian embassy. Everyone milled around while organizers entered the building with containers of kerosene. The police and fire department must have been in on it; they did nothing as the fires were lit. I was shocked by the breach in diplomatic immunity. "A lot of excitement, Mother, but be reassured that I was in no personal danger," I wrote. As in Syria, Nasser was hugely popular in Cairo, dominating the scene with "parades, patriotism, hatred of Israel, Pan-Arabism, helping other African nations, and Five Year Plans."

Over the next days, I kept up to date on the news with frequent trips to the magazine shelves at the library at the American Embassy. A cable for seventy-five dollars arrived from home, and I paid back my loan from the consulate. Unable to find a "poor-man's cafe," I splurged on a one-dollar kerosene camp burner and a frying pan to cook my own meals. I still wanted to travel around Europe before eventually making my way home, and cooking for myself would extend my cash reserves. After about three weeks, I set off once more. Next stop: Libya.

It took me four days to reach Benghazi. The hotels weren't just bad, they were also expensive, so I slept on police station floors. The Mediterranean Sea was to my right, and the sands of the Egyptian and Libyan coast stretched southward as far as you could see. All along the old, choppy asphalt road were reminders of the North African campaign of World War II: rusting gas cans, burnt-out tanks, ruined Jeeps. There were also several military cemeteries.

I rode 700 miles with the wind pelting my back with sand before turning south for the last eighty miles. "For once," I wrote, "it was actually a pleasure to ride the bike, with the wind behind me, it was almost a calm." I was probably half-joking when I wrote, "The bike and the weather are two entities I am very superstitious about; therefore I make my thanks conspicuous." I was vulnerable to the whims of both. Along the way I stopped at the well-preserved ruins of Cyrene, an ancient Greek, then Roman, city. I got a kick walking through the lanes between the ruins of houses, baths, and little amphitheaters. No one was around. Mosaic floors and walkways weren't protected. "It makes you feel you should wipe your feet before stepping on them," I wrote.

At a Salvation Army Hostel in Benghazi, I took my first bath in a week and a half, put in a bigger light bulb and planned my next move. The motorbike had gotten me far, but it was still another 1,100 miles to Tunis and I didn't want to push my luck. I'd heard that for nineteen dollars you could buy a ticket on a ship from Benghazi to Italy. Depending on how well the motorbike ran, I could make Rome my next "rest" stop.

Finding passage aboard a ship, either as crew or as a paying passenger, was harder than I anticipated; so was trying to sell the motorbike. I moved into a "not-so-cheap and not-so-clean hotel" (it had bedbugs) and spent my afternoons at the harbor, sitting in the sun and reading *Typee* by Melville and *Tortilla Flat* by Steinbeck. At night I cooked dinner in my room.

On my drive to Benghazi, I had seen a stream of British army convoys that stretched from the coast all the way down to the city. The British and Americans were all over the place, working in the oil industry or stationed at nearby military bases. The foreign military and its economic influence was strong. The Libyans almost seemed like second-class citizens in their own country.

No one, least of all other Americans, was used to seeing a poor American student. They were wary around me, afraid that I might put the touch on them. One day I met a man named Abdullah, a houseboy for an American couple, and he convinced me to come to his employers' house with him. The couple put me up in a room across the hall from Abdullah, but it was awkward. "Now, Henry, don't you let him take the lead in this thing," I overheard the wife, Mrs. Morse, whisper to her husband. I was embarrassed and uneasy. After that, I found it was easier to keep my distance from Americans. I spent a week in the company of British ex-pats, but that was no better. I felt better when I moved to the Arab quarter.

"Depression due to circumstances which you can't control (as opposed to one's personality) is soon over when circumstances change," I wrote home. I had reason to be happy. That morning, the captain of a small Dutch freighter had agreed to take me—and my motorbike—to Italy for thirty dollars. He didn't want me bringing any bugs on board, so before I was allowed on the ship I had to help the engineer douse my belongings with DDT. Aside from that, the captain ran things in an informal way. His wife and one of their children were with him. In the shallow channel north of Sfax, Tunisia, we dropped anchor and went for a swim, the captain with his aqualung strapped to his back. It was great fun. They also let me take the ship's wheel a couple of times. The second time was during rough seas, when the boat pitched and rolled so much that I nearly got sick. With each gigantic wave, the bow rose straight up in the air, then came down with a violent smack, shaking everything in the boat, including the ship's compass. The wheel almost tipped me over, and I found it impossible to stay on course.

Meals weren't as good as on an American ship, but the food, mostly bread and potatoes, was plentiful. The crew teased me about how much I ate. Most of the time I lay in bed, read, or played chess with the captain. I hadn't realized how hard life had been before I came on board. Too little food, too little conversation, too many things to be wary about. Having

Europeans to talk to made me feel less homesick. It was nice to not have to feel on guard all the time.

In Bizerte, Tunisia, I had the chance to return to the States on the SS *Ike*, a World War II Liberty ship, working for my passage as a galley boy. I was tempted, but I wasn't homesick enough to give up the idea of riding the motorbike through Europe. Near the end of March, I wrote in my journal: "Now we are passing close along the coast of mountainous Corsica. There's snow on the mountain tops which seems strange in contrast to the sunny weather we have been having since Bizerte. Beautiful country—I can see why immigrants to the States were homesick. One sees little villages perched halfway up the mountain sides and the whole coast rolls by as if we were on a train. Yesterday it was Sardinia passing by us. The captain stopped the ship by some fishing boats to trade cigarettes for fish—turned out to be mostly shrimp. I got a kick out of our stopping at each of three smallish boats where I heard the captain giving official type orders down to the engine room with the telegraph bell ringing for half speed, full stop, half astern, all so the captain could hold up a carton of Chesterfields and see if the boat had some fish."

CHAPTER FOURTEEN

From Europe to Home

The motorbike was in desperate need of an oil change, a new chain, and at least one new tire, but I didn't want to spend the money since I planned to sell the bike in Austria. Ignoring the repairs, I rode south 300 miles from Genoa to Rome. The city was full of young people, especially Americans and Germans, and my hostel was clean, comfortable, and served cheap meals, wine included. I sent off a letter to my parents at the American Express office, informing them of my plans to travel through Germany, France, and England. I had originally hoped to get to Russia, but that wasn't possible anymore, not just because of my short supply of money, but because I'd gotten word that I was expected back at work at Jones Pass.

At the youth hostel, I met a Belgian girl, Nicki Voit, and we spent a couple of days zipping around the city in her little white sports car, a gift from her grandfather. She was in Italy with her sister and we enjoyed an innocent little romance. In a letter home, I wrote that she was "kind of a spoiled brat."

Rome was full of student tourists, and most of us seemed to be short on money. I met some Germans who were selling their blood to finance their travels. I wasn't that broke, but I did feel lucky when a local offered to treat me and a couple of other Americans to a cup of coffee at an expensive cafe. The feeling evaporated after he stranded us with the bill. I was more street-smart when a local told me and a couple of Australians that he would drive us around town. He pretended to go fetch his car, then returned to ask for money to get it out of the garage. The Australians were reaching into their wallet when I called them off.

After a few days in Rome, I left for Florence, this time traveling with an English guy, both of us on motorbikes. When the expected happened and my chain broke, he gave me one of his spare links (something I hadn't thought to get for myself) to repair it.

Florence had a different feel than Rome. I wasn't as impressed by its architecture but appreciated its history. Everyone from Machiavelli to da Vinci to Galileo had some sort of tie to Florence. I went to the main art gallery with an Australian painter, and he gave me a lesson on the history of painting. Two days of Botticelli and Titian was plenty. I left Florence and rode to Venice. The only thing I wrote in a letter home about that city, aside from a comment on the church domes, was the fact that you didn't have to watch out for cars, since there weren't any.

From Venice I rode over the Brenner Pass and through the Dolomite Alps, a breathtaking journey. By Innsbruck, I was ready to go home. The long months of being on my own, on my guard, and feeling like my fate wasn't in my hands (it's hard to feel in charge when you don't know the customs, language, or local currency), had worn thin. I was no longer "captain of my soul," and wouldn't be until I was back on home turf.

It was a huge relief to finally sell the motorbike. I pocketed the seventy-two dollars, packed up my stuff, and made my way to the highway leading to Munich. Just as I stuck out my thumb to catch a ride, a VW van stopped. A couple of students from St. Louis University, Catholic pacifists, were touring Europe, and they stopped for anybody looking for a ride. I spent the night in the van debating sociology, jammed between an American girl and a scroungy German hitchhiker. "How can you begin to measure something like love with a yardstick or meter readings?" they asked. I argued that we could still hope for an understanding that is broadly "scientific." However, I was unconvinced by my own argument. In a letter home, I wrote: "I was so eloquent in defining sociology, I really wish all I hope for in the field is true."

The next day, I was on the road in Strasbourg, thumbing my way to Paris. I wasn't in any particular hurry, but I was tired of sleeping in police stations and cheap hotels. Now that I was getting accustomed to the ease of car travel again, I had even less patience. After going only fifty miles in three hours, I broke down and bought a train ticket in Sarrebourg. I stretched across three empty seats and slept until the train pulled into the Gare de l'Est station.

In Paris, the newfound feeling of freedom—no more motorbike to worry about!—gave way to the usual frustration of finding a place to stay. I ran around "like a dust mote with Brownian movement" before giving up on youth hostels and renting a hotel room on the Left Bank. At least I wouldn't have to pay to take the subway. I was already where I wanted to be.

The area was popular with American travelers, and my hesitation at talking with them returned. "A drawback to the Left Bank is that I'm always passing other Americans all dressed in ragged clothes carrying big folders presumably containing their art work. They know I am American by my clothes and we both seem embarrassed and look away not daring to mumble a hello or ask who you are."

I spent the next week enjoying the warm sunshine and the free park benches "often absent in other cities, evidently to discourage bums like me from camping on them." I visited the Louvre and the Musée d'Orsay and climbed the Eiffel Tower. I read Galaxy Science Fiction magazines bought from a used bookstore and the *New York Herald Tribune*, where I learned that the Soviets had launched a man into orbit. I had brought my ninth-grade French textbook, but my effort to brush up on my language skills was half-hearted. Mostly, I enjoyed settling into my tiny closet room with the *Herald Tribune* or a good Clifford Simak story and a breakfast of a baguette with margarine, cheese, and jam.

Spring was in full force, and I envied the couples necking on park benches in the afternoon sun (though "I would prefer evenings," I wrote home). I met an American girl, Betsy, and we went to a popular—and expensive—underground medieval restaurant to eat and listen to French folk songs. Betsy had agreed to pay half, but when the seven-dollar check came, I was left footing the whole thing. The next day I went to her place and asked her for three dollars and fifty cents. It was an uncomfortable moment for both of us.

In general, I noticed that Paris and the bohemian scene was easier to navigate for girls. Referring to a Canadian girl, I wrote: "She is cute and therefore getting into the inner circle of 'artists' here; for example, going to parties for the novelist Henry Miller (whose books are banned in the States). I don't have much of a chance because usually male 'artists' outnumber females two to one and outnumber cute females about five to one...."

After a week of being in Paris, it was time to move on. Just as I reached the highway to hitchhike out of town, Peter Nelson, my roommate on the ship coming over, drove by in his new VW bug. I had been intending to hitchhike to Cologne, but instead I joined Peter and Lynn Hall, a quiet artist friend from high school, on their way north through Holland to Bremen. After driving straight through Belgium, we stopped and slept, uncomfortably, in the VW; outside it was cold and wet. From there we made our way towards Bremen, which we reached after spending one night at the Zuiderzee.

I was surprised by all the rustic countryside in Germany; I hadn't expected so many forests and farms. "Only when you see statistics and witness the industrial side of Germany do you realize what a rich country it was and even more so now is," I wrote. Another unexpected sight were the convoys of US army vehicles on the highways and trains loaded with US tanks. After we dropped Lynn off in Frankfurt, Peter and I drove the winding back roads through the hilly Rhone countryside to the Sinntal Bruderhof in northern Bavaria. We were both running low on money, and I knew they would host us.

I was surprised to find many of the people I'd known in Paraguay there, including Georg, my former teacher, and Bob Peck, a young American member I had helped in the gardening department. The group was in the process of closing up its Paraguay community. There were no Arnolds at Sinntal. In a letter home, I wrote: "The Martin family seemed to be at the helm with Arno as Servant and Mrs. as head of the kitchen. I enjoyed meeting and re-making acquaintances with really open and good people like the Fischley man, Roland Keiderling, and Gerhardt Wieman (from Isla). These three and Otto told me particularly to greet the family and especially you, Dad. Fischley and Roland told me all about the celebration with your hot dog machine and the pie throwing which everyone got a big kick out of. Roland's wife (I forgot her name) wants to hear from you, Nancy, and may write to you—I gave her your address."

Bob Peck seemed apprehensive when we mentioned that we might stay a week, but we were shown the typical Bruderhof courtesy and given a place to sleep in a room with Albert, the old Loma horse driver.

For the next few days, we took sledgehammers to the large stones dumped by a truck behind the workshop preparing for a driveway. We also worked on a garden project and helped several pretty girls in the kitchen with the after-meal cleanup. We enjoyed ourselves. It had been ten years since my family's stay at the Bruderhof, and what struck me now with absolute clarity was how essential the belief in Jesus Christ was to the Bruderhof life.

After three days, Peter and I cut our visit short; we'd had enough of the hard work of breaking rocks. At dinner I made up a story about why we had to leave. No one bought it, and they all laughed. I was embarrassed and resolved to avoid lying in the future.

Peter and I spent the next few nights sleeping in the car, too lazy and broke to find a hostel. Despite the austerity measures, the money from selling my motorbike was dwindling fast. I asked my parents to send money "right away." "I should plan ahead more," I wrote, "but it is exciting sometimes to be a slave to outrageous circumstances." I bought a twelve-dollar train ticket to Dover. Except for a pittance, my money was gone.

After a brief stay in Dover (the proverbial white cliffs really are white), I arrived in London, where I found a room at an East End hostel and a stack of mail waiting for me at the American Express office. There were letters that had been forwarded from Rome and Paris, a forty-dollar check from my parents, and a seventy-six-dollar tax refund. "I'm in the bucks again!" I wrote home. I had a return ticket for the *Newfoundland*, but its departure date had been pushed back. To get home in time (almost) for my job at the Denver Water Board, I refunded my *Newfoundland* ticket and used the money, plus an extra nineteen dollars, for passage aboard Cunard's *Mauritania*.

With nearly three weeks to go before my departure, I decided to hitchhike up to the north of England to visit Mike Williams, a student I had met in Innsbruck. Mike was doing his graduate studies at Durham University. Durham is a charming small city near Newcastle, complete with castle, cathedral, and a river running through the center of town. Mike and his roommates rented rooms in an old house, and I spent the next five days there, sleeping on a mattress on the floor (a luxury after all the anonymous hotels), talking to the guys, wandering around town. The cathedral put me in a contemplative mood. While walking slowly underneath the high, vaulted ceilings, I wondered what it must have meant to peasants doing the same thing eight hundred years before.

After five days, I hitchhiked up to Scotland, where I saw my first live musicals, *West Side Story* and *My Fair Lady*. I wandered through the mountainous terrain, stopping to look at the lochs. There wasn't much traffic on the back roads—a couple of times I walked five miles or more before I got a lift. A lot of young people from Edinburgh and Glasgow were roaming around during their week-long school vacation, so I didn't feel isolated. I couldn't always understand their thick accents. In one hostel, I listened to a group of twelve-year-old schoolboys without even catching the drift of their conversation. "I would enjoy meeting Scottish people more if they didn't try so hard to be Scottish, rolling their 'r's' and choking on their guttural consonants," I complained in a letter. My long months of travel were wearing on me. It was time to go home.

During my trip, I was cold, lonely, tired, poor, and hungry. I complained in one letter to my parents, "Believe me, many times during the last few days I would have given anything to be sitting around the kitchen table back home." But I also experienced moments of enjoyment and even exhilaration, like when I was heading south in Greece and saw Mt. Olympus in the distance.

Some people go into the army to get focused and settle into life; for me, it took a journey on a Puch. My trip was a chance to go out into the world before buckling down and getting serious about studies. When I got back, I was ready for school. And that was a good thing, because it would take the better part of the next decade for me to finish.

CHAPTER FIFTEEN

Back to School

The summer at Jones Pass was uneventful. On my days off, I helped with ongoing home repair projects at my parents' house. It was a family affair, with my sisters and their husbands—Mimi and Whitney had decided to marry—also pitching in. Dennis wasn't around much; he and Carla got married that summer. My father officiated at the wedding.

Back at CU in the fall, I moved into a small duplex on Water Street with Tim Kiovski. He had spent the previous year abroad, working in a factory in Germany. Neither of us were in with the fraternity crowd, but we had fun hosting occasional parties at our house. We brewed our own beer and charged money to raise funds for YPSL—eighteen-year olds were allowed to drink 3.2 beer back then—and hoped that girls would show up. Joyce Kramer, a friend from my early days in Denver, helped with the beer brewing and later told me how appalled she was that I used one of my socks to hold the hops. A couple of times the bottles exploded, spewing a sticky mess all over our sparsely furnished duplex. We switched to buying beer.

That semester, both Tim and I started dating German exchange students. I spotted Ruth Federschmidt first, in the cafeteria of the student union. Based on her unshaven legs—dark hair smashed in every direction under her nylon stockings—I knew she must be German. I struck up a conversation, trying out my pig German, but Tim beat me to the punch and asked her out first. After a few dates, I stole her back. It seemed she preferred the language I'd learned at the Bruderhof and at Park to the coarse, colorful German Tim had picked up at the factory. He found another German girl, Helga, who bossed him around considerably, although he seemed not to mind (they later married). I brought Ruth home with me for some skiing, and she joined my family for Thanksgiving.

I went home often, and much of the time was spent helping my parents convert their upstairs into a rental unit. We plastered, hung drywall, repaired the porch, and lowered the ceiling in the living room. We removed the inside stairs and built an exterior staircase, and I put an antenna on the roof for FM radio (a couple of years later, I would add a rooftop antenna for a ham radio). Dad and I took out a load-bearing wall to enlarge the living room. Using a system of pulleys and jacks, we installed a fifteen-foot steel beam to support the second floor.

A highlight of the summer: Julia Hayhoe, the daughter of my mother's half-sister Dorothy, visited from Minneapolis. She was a flight attendant two or three years older than me, and beautiful.

Back at school, I got more involved in social activism. Boulder wasn't exactly a hotbed of civil rights protests, but people began organizing demonstrations at the local Woolworths, and I joined in. CU had a wonderful event called Public Affairs Week, with guest speakers and rallies. When it took place that spring of 1962, I stood on a corner outside the student union and expressed my views on Vietnam, a place previously unfamiliar to me and to most people. The war there was heating up, and I was against US involvement. A small crowd gathered to listen, and when I finished, a couple of young women approached me. Nancy Sand and Joanne Fox were friends from New York who recently had moved to Boulder. Joanne, a nurse, was an attractive young woman with dark hair and a free spirit. Nancy was a legal secretary. They rented a motel cabin at the edge of town near Boulder Canyon and worked on campus, Nancy at the law school and Joanne at the campus health center. Joanne was taking some classes, but mostly the girls were in town to have fun.

They frequently hosted parties at their cabin, and I became a regular. They were awkward affairs where the guys stood around staring at each other; no women were invited. Gradually, the other guys stopped coming around, leaving me to pursue Joanne. Nancy dated Ray Prach, a part-time student who supported himself as a waiter. He wasn't as ambitious as she would have liked—she was accustomed to lawyers—but she overlooked it. She and Joanne were awed by the mountains and by living in Colorado. I was too used to Colorado to feel this way, but Joanne and Ray were like Nancy—thrilled to be living in Boulder. We became a tight foursome.

To celebrate my upcoming graduation, my parents offered to buy me a car. Their upstairs tenant was selling a twelve-year-old Studebaker, but I had my heart set on a foreign car. Joanne and Nancy both drove VW bugs; I thought they were beautiful, but they were too expensive. I settled on a $150 ten-year old Hillman Husky, a small British two-door station wagon. The fact that it didn't run—or even start—didn't bother me. I borrowed some tools from Tim and went to work. With the car parked two wheels on the street and two on the curb, I had just enough room to crawl underneath and pull back the bell housing to expose the

Ed's first car, a ten-year-old Hillman Husky prone to overheating on mountain inclines.

ring gear on the fly wheel. The teeth of the ring gear were badly worn—the reason the car rarely started—but flipping it over and popping it back onto the flywheel solved the problem.

That was not the only problem with the car. In August, I was driving up a long hill in the mountains on my way to the Salida claim when the car overheated. The combination of the day's high temperature and the high altitude had caused the gasoline to turn into vapor in the fuel line—vapor lock. I had to leave the car and walk some miles to the cabin.

To keep it from happening again, I devised a crude but effective solution. I borrowed a Mason jar from my mother, added water, and drew two plastic tubes through a sealed lid. I fastened the jar in the engine compartment, snaking one tube through the dashboard near the steering wheel and pointing the other tube towards the fuel pump. When I drove up the mountain roads, I kept my mouth on the tube and blew when the engine threatened to overheat; under the hood, water dribbled through the other tube onto the fuel pump, cooling it. Problem solved.

That spring, I took an entrance exam for graduate school. Dad recorded in his journal: "His score on Graduate Record Exam: Social Science 99+; Natural Science 99+; Humanities 93; Sociology 99+. Fabulous! What hath we and God wrought?" I was pleased with my scores, but the moment of triumph that sticks with me most had to do with a project I completed for Professor Rose's class. Edward Rose was an off-beat, somewhat eccentric sociology professor. One of our assignments was to create an imaginary world; Professor Rose and his graduate students would describe these "worlds" in an experimental language they developed and record the results.

My inspiration came from Easter eggs I recalled from childhood: hollow, intact shells with a small peep hole to view the inside. I took an aluminum laundry case (the kind college students use to mail their dirty clothes home), painted the inside black, and drilled dozens of small holes in its surface. Inside, I stacked a beer glass and a casserole lid on top of a mirror. For the eyepiece, I installed a black-painted toilet paper tube.

When finished the results were fabulous. A viewer saw light looking like stars bouncing off the mirror and glassware in the inky blackness inside the box. Professor Rose loved it. He not only gave me an A for the course but also a recommendation for graduate school.

I graduated in the spring of 1962 with honors and a BA in sociology. I'd been a little sick of school before my big trip, but now I was back on track and excited about starting graduate work. The timing was good. With President Kennedy in office, there was a big push in government to boost medical and health education, and suddenly, fellowships were available for related disciplines like sociology. CU offered me one of these National Institute of Mental Health fellowships, but I wanted to study someplace with a national reputation. When the University of Michigan at Ann Arbor offered me the same thing, I accepted.

I spent the summer as an intern at the Colorado Psychopathic Hospital, walking the halls and talking with patients on a locked female ward, gathering data for a required paper. This wasn't like the big state mental hospitals where my parents had worked a decade earlier, but rather a well-funded, well-staffed university institution. I felt superfluous.

I was still seeing Joanne in Boulder when I started dating Ann Nordenbos, a nurse at the hospital. I'm not sure why I went out with her. Maybe I didn't want to make the thirty-mile drive to Boulder to see Joanne, or maybe it was another skirmish in the never-ending battle of the sexes; Joanne, I knew, was dating someone else, too. I told her about the relationship, but because she and Ann knew each other, I lied and said I was dating a Japanese exchange nurse. It was a silly lie and I'm not proud of it.

> *Bob Dylan sloped onto the scene. You said listen. I said 'awful.' Yet another thing you believed, way off the mainstream. ...And now Bob Dylan is awarded the Nobel in Literature. Deserved on the part of Dylan...courage on the part of the Nobel committee...and foresight on the part of Ed Sabin. What would we do without outsiders?*

— *from a 2018 email from a graduate school classmate, Fred Campbell*

CHAPTER SIXTEEN

Slogging Through

In Ann Arbor, Mimi and Whitney were leasing a Tudor style house from a faculty member who was away for the year, and I rented their spare room for my first few months at school. I buried myself in the library, mostly to study but sometimes to leaf through the library's old boating magazines and daydream about what kind I would own myself someday.

I got to know Fred Campbell and Ed Siva when we joined the same preliminary exam study group. A year ahead of me at school, they had entered grad school before the NIMH started handing out fellowships, so while I was a full-time student with no teaching responsibilities, they had to teach introductory sociology classes half-time to earn their keep. I looked up to both of them. Fred, more astute than me in the ways of academia, apprenticed himself to a big gun in the sociology department—I think it was Dudley Duncan—and went on to have a successful academic career at the University of Washington. At the time, I didn't realize the importance of finding a professor to take me under his wing. I had no mentor and not enough sense to look for one.

Politically, there was more going on than there'd been at CU, particularly off-campus. I participated in several "teach-ins" and "sit-ins" to protest the Vietnam War, and I joined the "Hands Off Cuba" march in New York and a war protest in Washington, DC, that drew a crowd of 25,000. Back in Ann Arbor, after a sit-in at the draft board office, I was charged with trespassing and sat in the county jail for ten days.

Joanne Fox sees Ed off at the Denver train station for his return to Ann Arbor.

I also made several trips to Boulder to visit Joanne, driving twenty-four hours straight with only short naps on the side of the road. I saw my parents, but I usually slept on the floor of Joanne and Nancy's apartment in Boulder. During my first year of grad school, I brought Joanne home over Thanksgiving to meet my parents. A year later, as I was making the same trip (this time in my Triumph TR3, the used sports car I bought partly with funds from my stipend), I noticed cars pulling off the road somewhere in Iowa. I stopped to ask what was going on. President Kennedy had been shot.

My interest in mental health may have originated with my mother and discussions during the time she was taking a class in abnormal psychology. Can people really be crazy? Are mental disorders real, or just a convenient way of labeling people who fall outside the norm, who are different, disreputable? Maybe crazy was just a group reaction to people outside the mainstream? Those were questions going around in my mind, and I wanted to make it my focus of study at Michigan. But no one on the faculty specialized in this branch of medical sociology, and there weren't any ongoing research projects going on there on the subject.

Michigan had an interdisciplinary program in social psychology, another interest of mine and one of the reasons I had opted to do my graduate studies there. The program was chaired by Theodore Newcomb, the author of the textbook for my social psych course at Park College. The program was selective, however, and I didn't make the cut.

I knew I wanted to study sociology, but I had a hard time settling on a particular focus. For a grad student, I was naive. I wrongly assumed that this was an extension of undergraduate school, a time to explore and discover what I really wanted to study. I flitted from one class to another, like a bee tasting each flower. I dropped one class as soon another caught my interest.

It was almost as though I had an urge to self-destruct. One example was the experience I had taking a human ecology seminar with Amos Hawley. The goal of the seminar was to apply to sociology the same methods used in the hard sciences, with studies based on population, geography, economics, etc. I'm not sure it wasn't a spoof, but I remember one thought experiment that described the various angles of people fleeing from a machine gun fired into a crowd. We used Hawley's textbook, *Human Ecology*, which I thought was pretty informative compared to some of the more theoretical sociology books I had to read. Hawley warned us that he didn't want to debate the relative merits of his approach to other more squishy areas in sociology, such as social psychology or social theory, since he had been having this quarrel for years at the University of Michigan. So, of course, what did I do but raise that very same question about the merits of his approach in our seminar. I got a C+ for the course, a bad grade in graduate school.

And then there was my class with Guy Swanson, the department chair. He gave us a take-home final exam on Talcott Parsons, a leading sociological theorist at Harvard University. Parsons' books were impenetrable to me, partly because I failed to beat my head against them enough to penetrate them, but also because of their apparent simplicity. I couldn't follow the arguments he was making. My plan was to make up for all the work I had not done with one final push the night of our exam. At the time, I was dating Judy, an English teacher studying for her master's degree. When she showed up at my apartment that evening, making love to her seemed more important than faking my way through the exam.

By the end of my third year, I had finished all my coursework and passed my prelims (or nearly so; I had to write a paper because of a conditional pass on one prelim). But I still hadn't grasped the fact that graduate school was like an apprenticeship, and that I needed to attach myself to a faculty member with the clout and know-how to steer me through the process. I had given up the idea that I could bounce from subject to subject, but now I was under the illusion that grad school—and my dissertation—was a chance to dig deep into an area of study and make my mark.

Professor Swanson (or, as I liked to call him, "the smiling hangman") called me in for an interview. By then I had been receiving the NIMH fellowship for three years, and he wasn't sure I deserved it for a fourth. During our meeting, he asked me what I perceived to be a standard trick question: Why did I feel that, historically, England produced exceptional writers, France exceptional painters, and Germany exceptional music? I drew a blank and was tempted to offer a sophomoric sociological answer: How did we know this was true? Maybe each culture had merely convinced the rest of the world of this superiority—after all, who can account for fads and fashions? However, I held back that answer. Because I couldn't think of anything else to say, I remained silent.

Thanks to that interview and my spotty grades, I lost the NIMH fellowship. I was given a teaching fellowship but lost that after one semester as well. I took a position as a part-time instructor at Eastern Michigan University in nearby Ypsilanti to support myself.

After two years of dating, I broke up with Judy. As with so many of my relationships, I was afraid that I was standing in her way of finding someone to settle down with. Like a coward, I never told her this was the reason for the breakup.

At the same time, my relationship with Joanne continued on and off. During a previous summer break, I followed her to Chicago, where she had moved with Nancy to be near another guy she liked, a student at the University of Chicago. I spent the summer working as a recreation aide at a Chicago housing project.

Earlier Joanne had invited me to visit her at her parents' home in Florida, and it didn't go well. When her mother asked me what I wanted to do after school, I said, half-jokingly, "I want to be a hobo." I was working my ass off to earn a PhD and become a sociologist, so it seemed pretty apparent that I didn't really want to become a bum, but her mom didn't get it. Things got even worse after that. One morning, Mrs. Fox wondered when Joanne was going to get up. I went into her bedroom to wake her. Mrs. Fox was appalled. In her view, a man had no business entering her daughter's bedroom. Joanne and I weren't sleeping together—our relationship never reached that point—but the incident caused trouble between her and her mom. Joanne thought her mom should know she wasn't doing anything wrong. She believed people should have faith in her without her needing to explain herself.

She and I were considering marriage, but we were never ready for it at the same time. In Boulder, on a sudden impulse, I proposed. I hadn't bought a ring or considered how I would support us. I didn't want to think it through, I just wanted to get married. She turned me down, saying she had promised her mother that she would never elope and that when she married, it would be with a proper ceremony. She was right. That would have been a bad way to start a marriage.

Things dribbled on at a low level after that. She dated some other guys, one of them a business major I'd met briefly in Colorado, Kai Helding. On one of her visits to Ann Arbor, she told me Kai had proposed to her. The question on her mind was clear: Should she marry him, or wait for me? By then I had grown cold feet, not just about marrying her, but about marrying in general. My future seemed like a journey that hadn't come into focus yet, and I didn't know where it would lead me.

Could I really ask a woman to come with me when I didn't know where I was going? It was a question that would bother me over the next decade.

I doubt that things would have worked out for us, even if I had been ready. Joanne was similar to her Finnish-American father in that she was reserved, and she expected me to understand intuitively the things she left unsaid. Neither of us was good at sharing our feelings about what was going on inside. Today, after four decades of marriage, I know how important it is to communicate well. I don't think Joanne and I would have made it, although I'm happy to say that she and I are still in touch these many years later.

As a PhD candidate, I should have chosen a small piece of a subject already being researched at Michigan, something that one of the professors had an interest in that I could assist him in. But I didn't realize that at the time. Not doing this made completing my dissertation more difficult. I needed empirical data to analyze for my dissertation, and I finally settled on studying a portion of a national survey on family interaction, done by the Survey Research Center on campus. Stupidly, I had failed to take the only course on the family offered by the department, a class taught by Robert O. Blood.

I cobbled together a PhD committee and got my proposal approved. It wasn't much, but it was enough to get me started. After four years in Michigan, I was eager to move. I should have stayed a fifth year to make some progress on my dissertation, but I couldn't stand the thought of another Ann Arbor winter. At the end of the term, in June 1966, I packed up my belongings and headed for a new teaching position at Kansas State University in Manhattan, Kansas.

CHAPTER SEVENTEEN

Small Town Teaching

eaving Ann Arbor so soon was a mistake, but I didn't know it yet. I had a dissertation topic, but just barely. I had no real mentor, and I was working hundreds of miles away from the university. I had plenty of data to analyze from the Survey Research Center, but the only professor in my area of study—Professor Blood—wasn't on my dissertation committee.

My position as assistant professor of sociology at K-State paid $10,000 per year, a good salary. I moved into Wildcat Creek Apartments, a new complex at the edge of town, and bought furniture from a departing faculty member. In Ann Arbor, the axle had broken on my Triumph, and I had traded it in for a four-door Renault Dauphine. Now, feeling flush, I splurged on a silver 1967 Corvette Stingray, the first new car I ever owned. I also bought a used Honda motorcycle, which I soon upgraded to a new 500cc Triumph, a wonderful English bike. And I sent money home, thirty dollars at a time, to repay all the loans my parents had given me over the years. They accepted at first, but after a year they told me to stop.

Ed gives a ride to his niece, Mimi Nadya, on his Triumph Daytona 500 motorcycle. Behind them is the graduate student housing where Dan, Nancy, and their family lived. The Triumph was imported from England and of the several motorcycles Ed owned, this was his favorite.

My position was split between teaching and doing research. Medicare was rolled out the year I arrived at K-State, and Eugene Friedman, the department chair, was part of a team of researchers who'd been given a grant to assess the brand-new program. My job was to see how well it was working in Great Bend, Kansas, 150 miles southwest of Manhattan.

If I were going to do the research today, I would know just how to approach it. With a letter of introduction in hand, I would interview a hospital nursing supervisor, a doctor, nurses, a pharmacist and patients—anyone involved in Medicare who was willing to talk to me.

But that's what I know now, with decades of experience behind me. Back then I was a young PhD student wet behind the ears, intimidated by the thought of wandering around and talking to strangers. As a result, I avoided direct contact with the people I most needed to interview and instead spent my time and energy on data analysis, tabulating survey results that had been collected under contract by the project. It was a safe diversion, but I knew I wasn't doing the job justice. After two years, I resigned with the excuse that I needed more time to focus on my dissertation. I still had my half-time teaching job, but without the research, my salary was cut in half. I sold the Corvette and the Triumph motorcycle.

Even with all the new free time, I didn't expend much energy on writing my dissertation. I went through the motions but had no sense of urgency. Instead, I spent too much time chasing women, fooling around with photography, and, as always, daydreaming about boats.

Years earlier, I had taught myself to sail on a little Sunfish. Now, I spent my free days on a small homemade sailboat I had purchased, sailing

*Photo taken at family gathering in Idaho Springs circa 1968.
Standing, from left: Robin, Dan, Ed, Ray, Whitney, and Jesse.
Seated, from left: Billy, Alex, Nancy, Betty, Jason, Mimi, and Mimi Nadya.*

at nearby Tuttle Creek Lake. My dad shared my interest in boats, and he and I decided to build one together. We pooled our money and sent a check to Arthur Piver, a boat designer in California. A couple of weeks later, a thick sheaf of papers covered in tiny print came in the mail: the building plans for the Mariner, a 25-foot-long trimaran.

On Thanksgiving break in Idaho Springs, Dad and I cleared out the old horse stalls and troughs from the big shed behind their house and converted the space into our new boat shop (a step "in preposterousness," as Dad wrote in his journal). He may have been skeptical about our ability to build a twenty-five-foot plywood boat, but he didn't show it. The plans were solid, although they contained few diagrams. We sometimes puzzled over a single paragraph for a half-hour or more, scratching our heads and asking: "What the hell does that mean?" The only way to figure it out was to set up pieces; for example, boat frames on long wooden rails so we could visualize it.

Whenever I could get home, Dad and I worked on the boat. We cut out the frames and glued them together. Each one was successively bigger, so that as we layered them, they extended further back and then got smaller towards the stern. In this way, the hull, which we built upside down, grew larger in stages. In the winter, we used electric heaters and heat lamps in order for the glue and resin to cure properly.

Next, we bent large sheets of marine-grade plywood to cover the frames, attaching them with bronze boat nails and Resorcinol waterproof glue. We did the sides first, and then the top—which would be the bottom of the boat once we flipped it right side up. After coating the plywood with a polyester resin, we applied a layer of fiberglass, straightening and smoothing the sheets of glass cloth onto the sticky resin as we went along. The shed gave us plenty of room to work. Whoever got there first got to choose the radio station we listened to; Dad always picked classical, and I chose pop music.

Over the course of the next several years, the *Big Do* took shape. My dad had built model boats, but this was the first time either of us had built a full-size boat. When I wasn't in town, we kept up steady correspondence about the project, brainstorming our next steps and discussing which parts to buy. Dad worked on it some while I was away teaching, but most of the work we did together. It was a wonderful experience; I think he appreciated our time together as much as I did.

Throughout my life, whenever I move someplace new, it takes me six months or a year to settle in and feel confident enough to make new friends. That was true in Manhattan as well. I don't remember how I met Karen Henry, a divorced political science student. I didn't get the impression that she took the master's program she was in seriously, but she was smart, maybe smarter than me. Karen and I dated, and we spent a great deal of time with her friend Nancy and Nancy's boyfriend, Jack Walters, from Los Angeles. He was in the Army and worked as a cook at nearby Fort Riley.

As the oldest of the group by about five years, I felt a little out of step with their generation. They didn't have goals beyond hanging out and enjoying themselves, an attractive contrast to what I was doing (or, in the case of my dissertation, avoiding). Their lives seemed exciting. After some resistance on my part, they turned me on to pot, and later, LSD. Both were new and thrilling, but I didn't like the effects they had on me.

Karen wasn't just book-smart. She was intuitive and observant. For instance, she pointed out that every time we were heading to my apartment to make love, I would start singing the children's song "Hot Cross Buns" under my breath. She had to be pretty sharp to pick up a detail like that; I didn't even know I was doing it. She also knew how to play games at romance, how to inspire jealousy to keep someone interested in her.

What neither of us realized when we first started dating was that she was pregnant, the result of a previous relationship with an Irish exchange student. I shouldn't have gotten involved, but I was the only one with a car, so I volunteered to drive her and her previous boyfriend a hundred miles to Kansas City so they could tell her mother the news. Karen's mother and her father, a successful attorney, had divorced when Karen was a child. Sitting in her mom's nice suburban home, I tried to explain my part in this domestic drama—I had a car; I wasn't the father of the baby; I was Karen's boyfriend. Then Karen and her mother went around and around in circles, discussing what should be done. In general, shotgun marriages are not a good idea, but it surprised me how easily the Irish ex-boyfriend got off the hook. He felt some obligation to marry her, but the idea was rejected.

Maybe the whole thing had been a set-up; maybe Karen let me drive them in order to present me to her mother as a marriage prospect; why should she have to marry the Irish student if she could have me? I didn't know what was going on in her mind. At any rate, it was later decided that Karen would spend the rest of her pregnancy as a nanny for a family in Lincoln, Nebraska, and then give the baby up for adoption.

After she moved to Lincoln, things between us cooled. I visited her two or three times, but by the time she returned to Manhattan, I was seeing other people. Then she started hanging around a strange hippie guy. We spent time with each other, but it was a little unclear who was with whom. I think I was afraid of her getting into my mind and playing games.

Not that I was above playing games myself. In the one conversation Karen and I had about marriage, I was a little too frank. I told her that for me, getting married to her would be like sticking my hand into a meat grinder. She looked shocked for a moment and then laughed.

I didn't recognize it then, but I was following a well-established pattern. I loved the wonderful world of women, but I wasn't ready to settle down. I was still on my journey to an unknown but sparkling future, a journey I was convinced I had to travel alone. I would date someone for a while and then, knowing I didn't want to marry her and not wanting to stand in the way of her finding someone who did, I'd break it off. There's nothing wrong with the impulse to get out of the way for a marriage prospect, but I still regret, years later, not explaining the reason I felt I had to break up with these women. I should have been more honest.

Sometime after earning his PhD in 1968, Dan moved with my sister and their children to Salt Lake City, where he took a faculty position with the University of Utah's modern languages department. My parents followed them there three years later, but in the meantime, Dad and I continued working on the trimaran. During breaks from teaching, I would spend a week or more in Idaho Springs. In the summer of 1968, we planked and covered the hull with fiberglass, established the water line, and painted the bottom of the main hull and the pontoons with red epoxy. A year later we put up walls of the boat's cabin and installed bunks.

The boat progressed; my dissertation didn't. What I didn't understand at the time was that the purpose of the dissertation was to teach me how to use the tools of sociology, not for it to become the highlight of a life's work. I had little knowledge about how to complete a dissertation, and even less motivation.

Feeling guilty about disappointing Friedman on the Medicare project and wanting to move to a larger city, I applied and was accepted to teach at the University of Missouri in St. Louis (UMSL) in 1969.

CHAPTER EIGHTEEN

Back to City Life

It was exciting to return to a big city. I bought a used Oldsmobile large enough to pull a U-Haul trailer, packed up my stuff, and drove to St. Louis. I found a garden apartment in a redeveloped complex just east of St. Louis University. As usual, it took me some time to adjust to the new surroundings, and the first few months in St. Louis were lonely. I read Camus and Sartre. As one of the characters in Sartre's *Nausea* says: "Here we sit, all of us, eating and drinking to preserve our precious existence and really there is nothing, nothing, absolutely no reason for existing." I was still goofing off with my dissertation, but now I had a friend goofing off with me. Dick Ferrigno was another grad student teaching in the sociology department at UMSL and, like me, he wasn't doing much on his dissertation.

After a semester or so, I joined a faculty member from the political science department to do an experimental class in political sociology. We sat in a circle with the students and discussed issues. I worried that it would turn into a BS session—the kids got to grade themselves—but the political climate was running at a high temperature then, and the students seemed to get something out of the class, if nothing more than by listening to arguments between me and my fellow teacher. One of our students was a young, attractive, free-spirited woman named Gail Gaus. She worked as a hotel reservationist to put herself through school. My co-teacher confided in me that he was having an affair with her.

"What are you doing with a married guy?" I asked Gail. I wasn't just a teacher showing concern for a student. I wanted to knock the other guy out of the picture and date her myself. It wasn't ethical on my part, but at least I wasn't married.

It worked. Gail dropped him, and we started seeing each other. Her friend Cookie dated Mike, a Vietnam vet who lived a little on the wild side. He wasn't a student, but I invited him to sit in on the discussion class, and we became friends. The four of us spent a lot of time together.

Like me, Gail opposed the war in Vietnam. She and I drove on my Kawasaki motorcycle to a protest in Washington, DC, where we joined thousands of people on the Mall and listened to speeches played over loudspeakers. It was a peaceful demonstration, with plenty of portable toilets and Red Cross trucks. But by this point, our protests seemed futile; the war kept going on and on, regardless of thousands of people showing up for marches and demonstrations.

I spent Christmas break with my parents in Idaho Springs and worked on the boat. They had made friends with another retired couple, the Shallers. Mr. Shaller was conservative and a racist. When the couples got together to socialize or play bridge, he would talk about what he considered the inferiority of African Americans. My dad asked me for some arguments he could deploy when the topic came up, but I responded with a pseudo-scientific dodge, claiming there wasn't enough data or research to settle the question. Of course, I should have pointed out the obvious: Shaller was parroting the same views you see everywhere in the world when a member of the dominant group talks about a subordinate group. I still regret I failed my father in that regard.

In January, just one semester after my arrival in St. Louis, my car was stolen. In a strange way, that was the kick in the rear I needed. If I had my PhD, I reasoned, I would get a raise, and that would soften the blow of losing the car. Also, a five-year deadline was looming; if I didn't finish before then, I would have to take prelim exams all over again. It was a dreadful prospect.

My parents drove my old Renault, which I had stored at their house, to St. Louis, and I took off for Ann Arbor, where I spent the next day or two wandering up and down the halls of the sociology department in search of a professor who would agree to be my dissertation chairman. David Segal was a young professor in a different field, but he agreed to take me on. By this time, I had made some progress analyzing the survey data. Now it was just a matter of buckling down to write up the results.

Dick saw me making Xerox copies of a chapter or two of my dissertation, and that motivated him, too. We both got to work, and within a few months, both of us had finished. In July 1970, I got the phone call that my dissertation had been accepted. That December, halfway through my second year of teaching at UMSL, I was awarded a PhD. Not wanting to spend the time or money to go to Ann Arbor, I skipped the graduation ceremony.

In the spring of 1971, I turned in my resignation. I had no interest in sticking around now that I'd earned the degree. I gave up my apartment, bought a yellow school bus, parked it in a field in the suburbs, and moved in. Instead of planning my classes, I spent most of my free time planting a vegetable garden and fixing up the bus. It didn't have a working engine when I bought it, so I purchased a Ford motor from a wrecking yard, and Mike helped me install it. We took out most of the seats and replaced them with plywood beds. I got a Coleman stove, a washbasin, and jugs to store water. The great outdoors was our only toilet. As a final touch, we painted the exterior of the bus in rainbow colors. I was a late-blooming hippie with a beard who lived on a bus—no doubt UMSL was relieved to see me go at the end of the school year.

With events such as the bombing campaign in Cambodia and the shootings at Kent State, there was a growing sense of anger and futility among the public. In early May 1971, planners organized another march, this time with more aggressive tactics. Mike and I arrived in DC to join 35,000 protestors. We were encouraged to block major intersections and bridges in the hopes that disrupted traffic would have some effect. Each time police showed up at a blocked intersection, people ran off in every direction to start over at another spot. The crowd was like a blob; every time we were squeezed out of one area, we oozed into another. My trick was to run and then, as soon as I turned a corner, to walk slowly, pretending I was an innocent bystander.

The police staged a massive round-up, arresting 12,000 protestors, including Mike. Not knowing what had happened to him, I made my way back to the car and waited. It was the middle of the night when he showed up. He'd been released, along with almost everyone else, with a ten-dollar fine. In a letter home, I explained that Mike had been arrested, but I hadn't because "I ran faster than he did."

Betty pulling taffy with the grandchildren in Idaho Springs.
From left: Betty, Alex, Rob, Billy, and Mimi Nadya

That summer, Gail, Mike, Cookie, and I drove the bus to Colorado and spent the next few weeks working for my parents, building a retaining wall on rental property they had purchased across the creek from their house. At night, we slept in the bus. Nancy and her family were there, and Mimi came for a visit with her boys; it was a big crowd. We celebrated the Fourth of July with fireworks, and then Gail and

From left, Mike, Gail Gaus, and Ed at work on a retaining wall for Ray and Betty in Idaho Springs

Cookie left with two other UMSL friends for a trip to California, leaving Mike and me behind. I wanted to stay home and work on the boat.

By this time, Dad and I had been building the trimaran for several years, and I was eager to get it finished—not only because I wanted to get it on the water, but also because it was costing money. For example, we designed the boat so that the floats could be folded down to fit onto a trailer, and we had to spend sixty-four dollars for four custom-made

Ed standing on top of Big Do during final construction in Ray and Betty's back yard, summer 1971

stainless steel hinges. I wasn't employed anymore, and I wanted to make my money last.

In late August 1971, we hitched the boat and trailer to the back of the school bus and lumbered over Loveland Pass. That afternoon, my parents, Nancy and her family, and I christened the *Big Do* in Lake Dillon.

Ready for the maiden launch of Big Do at Lake Dillon, Colorado.
Paint on the bus courtesy of Mike, Ed, Gail, and Cookie in St. Louis.

CHAPTER NINETEEN

With the Trimaran to Texas

In September, my parents sold their house for $11,000 and moved to Salt Lake City. My mother was more eager to relocate than my dad. She wanted to be near Nancy and the kids. After I helped them move, I drove back to Idaho Springs and picked up the boat. I was going to be meeting Gail in Texas, where we planned to take the *Big Do* for a long cruise. She wanted to sail to Mexico; I wasn't so sure I wanted that much adventure.

Hauling the boat behind the school bus and driving thirty-five miles per hour, it took me several days to reach the Texas Gulf. The trimaran was of light construction, built more like an airplane than a boat, but even so, I wasn't confident the trailer could handle it. In Lubbock, I lost a few hours waiting for a broken spring bracket to be repaired at a machine shop; after that, I slowed down to a steady thirty mph. I still had 600 miles to go before I reached the Gulf.

After four days on the road, I arrived at Port Lavaca, a small town on a bay about twenty miles from the Gulf. The weather was cooler than I expected. I had purposely avoided the bigger port cities, because I wanted some practice on the water before I launched someplace more crowded. I was happy to find a boat ramp at a waterside park.

By the next day, I was missing the cool temperatures. The thermometer and the humidity rose in tandem, and by the time Gail arrived from St. Louis, the envelopes for my letters back home were sealing themselves shut.

On the way to Port O'Conner, we had trouble with trailer wheels. I repaired a flat tire, but one of the two wheels was breaking apart under the weight of the trimaran. For a boat, it didn't weigh much, but it was still too heavy for the single axle trailer. I wrote home to ask for $100 for a new axle and two wheels, and in return, I got a check for $150 and a letter from my mother, who was worried about us being in the deep South. I reassured her there was no danger from the Ku Klux Klan. "When I said it scares us," I explained of an earlier letter, "it was a scare about the Gulf, not bodily harm."

At Port O'Connor, we parked the bus near the Intracoastal Waterway, in a spot with a good view of the tugboats and barges chugging by day and night. It was too hot to sleep with the bus windows closed, and the mosquitoes swarmed us, impervious to all our insect strips and sprays. The next day I went into town and bought some screening for the windows.

Before Gail and I got in the water, our run of bad luck got worse. I was careful to put up the floats and the mast before I backed the *Big Do* down the boat ramp, but unfortunately, I didn't notice an overhead guy wire. Neither did Gail, who was outside the bus giving me directions. I got out and surveyed the damage. The wire had caught the mast and

"Boating is one minor crisis after another."
—my dad, quoting me in his journal

knocked it down. The forestay was broken, the masthead destroyed, and the mast itself bent, with the step ripped off. We wouldn't be sailing that day.

In the morning, Gail and I drove the bus into Corpus Christie to shop for replacement parts. We were able to buy a new forestay but not a mast. Back at the park, I used fiberglass to repair what I could and artfully (I hoped) jury-rigged the rest. Luckily, it worked. The next day, we sailed up the Intracoastal Waterway as dolphins raced alongside us, then left the waterway and sailed to an island sandwiched between the bay and the Gulf. Our next short excursion took place in the evening, when we sailed out to look at the buoys. On the way back, the wind slammed us into some rocks at the entrance to the Intracoastal Waterway, scraping the main hull and breaking the rudder. I was able to fix the rudder by swapping out the plywood blade with one made of steel.

Our next big challenge came when we tried to sail on the Gulf. The only way to get there was through a mile-long ship channel. Facing heavy winds, we tacked up the 150'-wide channel but didn't get far before the forestay came loose. Fortunately, the mast didn't come down with it, and we were able to sail downwind out of the channel and onto a beach. We spent the night anchored near the beach, with one line snaking out to a log on shore and another attached to an offshore anchor. In the morning, we tried again, but the big waves pushed us into the rocks. A fisherman with a big outboard motor saw us trying to walk the boat out of the channel and offered to tow us. After jury-rigging the rudder, we were able to sail downwind back to Port O'Connor.

"Mr. & Mrs. Sabin," Gail wrote in the margins of my letter home, "Isn't it wild all the trouble we've been having! I've discovered I'm a lousy sailor. [The waves made her seasick.] Ed is pretty good though, and none of these things have gotten him down. I've also discovered that I don't think I'll like being on the boat for long periods of time." That was written before we ever got on open water of the Gulf.

A few days later, we successfully made it out into the Gulf. The waves weren't as violent as they had been in the inlet, but they were still big enough to tip the boat considerably. Gail, seasick, stayed in the cabin, but I enjoyed the roller-coaster effect of the heaving waves. I had a chart showing the offshore oil platforms, and with a protractor and the chart's compass rose, I used them to steer our course, a method I'd learned from a shrimper. We were about five miles offshore. Each time I sighted a platform, I set course for the next one. We were making four knots; the jib halyard had become tangled when we launched that morning, and until I had a stable platform to untangle it, we had to rely on the mainsail.

Around 10 pm, just off Freeport, we got stuck. Try as I might, I couldn't locate the ship channel to get into Freeport. We cruised back and forth for an hour or more, trying to make sense of the different colors of lights on shore, until Gail convinced me to sail straight for the beach, where we found the channel and tied up to some old pilings. A horde of mosquitoes descended, and then the rain began to pour down. A steady stream of water leaked through a hole on Gail's side of the cabin. In the morning, the rain turned to a steady drizzle.

Leaving Freeport turned out to be even more difficult than getting there. The wind blew in from the northeast, the direction we wanted to sail. We tried tacking up to Galveston, but after six hours, we had only traveled six miles. At the end of the day, we gave up, exhausted.

All the troubles took their toll on us. Gail and I had stocked up on paperbacks, but even with reading as a diversion, we grew irritable with each other. I noticed a tendency in myself to boss her around, especially when I was scared—and I got scared every time we docked. Each time, the boat got a little more beat up. One of the books I bought, *A World of My Own* by Robin Knox-Johnston, wasn't a very good read, but it was about sailing around the world, and I ate up the technical details. Anything to help.

I'd like to say things got worse before they got better, but that's only partly true. They got worse, period. One night in mid-October, after we'd been taking turns sailing through the night, the wind suddenly died. I had run out of the large detail charts and had no way of identifying the heading for the harbor entrance. We made our way toward shore, tacking every fifteen minutes, and by the time we arrived at a jetty, which ran a half-mile out from the harbor, the wind was rising. We shouted to an approaching shrimp boat, asking if we could follow them in. It was hard to understand the captain over the howling wind and the drone of his motor, but we finally figured out that he was telling us to tie on to his boat. He was anchoring there for the night. Later, when the waves grew violent, he invited us to sleep in the cabin with his three-man crew. We curled ourselves into a single bunk in the hot, smelly, crowded cabin. I was so nervous about the *Big Do* that I got up repeatedly through the night to check on her.

By the morning, the wind had dropped, but the waves were coming high and fast. The captain predicted doom for the trimaran if we attempted to maneuver through the jetties while the tide was going out. He was bound and determined to rescue us, whether we wanted it or not. I agreed to let him tow us, although I knew my tow rope was too short (I must have been economizing when I bought it). The two boats got out of step, with the trimaran sliding down a wave faster than the shrimp boat went up the next, and they collided several times. The captain tried to remedy it by speeding up, but that only made things worse. Then, in one sickening moment, I watched as the tow rope yanked my boat downward from the top of a wave just as the shrimp boat came crashing down— right on top of it. It landed on the bow and snapped the front part of the port float off. The only thing keeping the two boats tethered together was a rope we had secured to the top of the cabin. I was sure the cabin would get ripped off, if the trimaran didn't sink first. Finally, the captain radioed the Coast Guard, who took over the job of towing us in. The water calmed down, and so did I. When we got to shore, Gail and I hitched a ride to a bus stop, then climbed on a bus back to Port O'Connor, where we picked up the school bus and trailer. Our trip was over.

SEARCHING FOR LIFE'S PURPOSE

October 26, 1971

Dear Mother & Dad,

Gail wants to go back to school next semester. I don't blame her—she is a senior and close to finishing. She is going back to St. Louis to get a job to save money for school. I want to visit a commune or two so I won't be along for a while. I want to repair the boat—maybe work for you all for room and board. I don't know what I'll do next—maybe go to Missouri to visit a commune there for a while.

No trouble so far towing the boat, but we have been driving really slow. Cold weather here which we thought we'd like but we don't—at least no flies or mosquitoes. The trip has been fun.

Your son, Ed

Why did I write that the trip had been fun? I didn't think so then, and I don't think so looking back on it now.

CHAPTER TWENTY

Late-Blooming Hippie

On November 2, I pulled into my parents' snow-covered driveway with the trimaran in tow. Now that the sailing trip had ended prematurely, I wasn't sure what to do with myself. A few days later, I packed some clothes, loaded my motorcycle onto the bus, and left for California. Besides wanting to visit Mimi and her family—Whitney was on the English faculty at Humboldt State University—I wanted to see some California communes I'd read about in *Mother Earth News*. The lifestyle appealed to me.

I knew that Joanne Fox—now Joanne Helding—was living with her husband in Stockton, so I contacted her and made plans to stop by for a visit. When I arrived, I parked the bus a street or two past her house, thinking it would save her some embarrassment. We were having a pleasant chat in her kitchen when she mentioned that her husband, Kai, would be home soon for lunch. It didn't register that this was my signal to leave. Without a car (or a rainbow-colored bus) to indicate my presence, Kai got a shock when he found a bearded hippie in bib overalls in the kitchen with

> *"You're either on the bus or off the bus."*
> —Ken Kesey

Ray inspecting the damaged bow section of Big Do's port pontoon after Ed hauled the boat back to Salt Lake City from the Texas coast

his wife. Joanne didn't bother to explain. Just as when I had known her earlier, she expected people to trust her even when the circumstances were odd. The atmosphere turned stiff and uncomfortable. After twenty minutes of stammering and trying to show that it was nothing but an innocent visit, I cut out. It was a bad scene.

After visiting a commune or two in California, I drove to the Morningstar Commune in New Mexico. It left me feeling cold—too large and impersonal. I thought back to Friendly Farm, the small commune Gail, Mike, Cookie, and I had visited in Norwood, Missouri, near the border of Arkansas. Wary of attracting too many hippies, Friendly Farm didn't do any advertising; they wanted to stay small. Compared to the others, this seemed like a good place for me.

By early December 1971, I was living in my (unheated) school bus at Friendly Farm. The community consisted of five men (with me, now six), two women, and a couple of children. I was the oldest by several years. On the grounds stood two ramshackle sheds heated by wood stoves, an old car or two, a small greenhouse, and a compost heap. We shared our food, including what I picked up at the grocery store with money I received from my tax return (getting a tax return and owning a motorcycle and a school bus made me the rich one of the group). I planted some seeds, hoping to get some seedlings started in the greenhouse for spring, but I didn't know what I was doing and killed them with too much watering. Judging by letters they wrote to each other at the time, my family was concerned about my apparent unhappiness (not Dan, though; he chalked it up to my dalliance with Eastern mysticism). In reality, I wasn't unhappy, just a little lonely and uncomfortable with the younger crowd.

One of the men wore funny clothes and was always cracking jokes; he never said it openly, but he implied that he'd been abused by staff at his Catholic school in Pennsylvania. It was the first time I'd heard of such a thing. One of the women was pregnant; the other lived on the commune with her young kids and mechanic boyfriend. She occasionally went off with another man, but always came back to the mechanic, who, despite being a high school drop-out, was a steady, responsible sort.

For fun, we took LSD, and I was reminded how much I disliked it. It intensifies everything: good music becomes great, tasty food becomes delicious, funny becomes hilarious. And if you're a little nervous to begin with, it turns your anxiety into paranoia. No, thanks.

I remained on the commune through the winter, and in early spring I organized a gardening initiative. Due to our inexperience, we chose an area under a giant oak tree. We tilled the ground, and I used a borrowed trailer to haul manure from a nearby dairy farm. None of us thought about what would happen once the tree leafed out. By the time we did, it was too late to relocate the garden. One of the men girdled the tree, a tactic once common among farmers to kill off a tree, and this sent the rest of the group into an uproar. They may not have been able to feed themselves off the land, but they were ecologically minded, and they let him have it mercilessly. I should have defended him, but I stayed out of it. He tried to undo the damage to the tree by covering the wound with tar, but I didn't stay long enough to see if it worked. Witnessing that kind of crazy interaction among people deflated my idealism; if you can't have peace and harmony in a commune, where can you?

By mid-May, I was on the road, making the long haul back to Utah. At the commune, I hadn't let them know my plans, and I felt bad about my sudden departure. I was adrift, with no firm plans about where I was going. I passed by a hitchhiker on the side of the road, and that made me feel even worse. Normally I stopped to pick them up, but I didn't want a stranger camping in the bus with me. He must have caught a ride with someone driving faster than me, because further down the road I saw him again. And then again. The last time I drove by, he flipped me off.

I spent the summer in Salt Lake City, working on my parents' house, repairing the trimaran, researching a book on anarchism that would never get written, and dating a teacher from Michigan named Sandy. Once the *Big Do* was repaired, we all went boating on Bear Lake, a large, deep mountain lake on the border of Utah and Idaho. I wrote to Arthur Stinchcombe, the chair of the sociology department at the University of California, Berkeley, telling him I wanted to study anarchism, and he offered me a quasi-fellowship: a university library card and the right to audit classes. That fall, I sold the bus for $350, packed what I could onto my Kawasaki motorcycle, and headed to California.

Second trip to California, to Berkeley via motorcycle, October 1972

CHAPTER TWENTY-ONE

Go West, Lost Man

The Vietnam War ground on and on and on; it was hard to imagine it ever ending. Anarchism had entered the zeitgeist. For liberals like me, it seemed like a solution.

I wasn't drawn to the radical, bomb-throwing version of anarchism, but instead to a more philosophical version, one that held a fundamentally optimistic view of humankind. If we could get rid of policemen, armies, and jails, the institutions that were warping our nature, we could live in peaceful, voluntary association with each other. It was a line of thinking influenced, no doubt, by my time on the Bruderhof and certainly by the communes, but mostly by the Vietnam War. I couldn't get past the idea that governments and the wars perpetuated by them were evil. If we got rid of a government based on force, we could get on with our natural state: living in harmony with each other.

There were critics of this kind of idealized thinking, but at the time I didn't agree with them. Later, I recognized that humankind hasn't evolved enough to live without the force of law to keep us in check. Government, though it has its dark side, is a necessary component of society.

In Berkeley, I moved into an apartment on Parker Street with Benjamin, the son of Egyptian Jewish emigrants. I had some money, but as usual, the challenge was to live as cheaply as possible. I attended lectures and hung out at the library. Through it all, my feeling of aimlessness persisted.

My dad and I had talked about selling the trimaran and had even gotten a response to our classified ad in the *Salt Lake Tribune*, listing it for $2,800. But neither of us was ready to part with *Big Do*. Borrowing Nancy and Dan's station wagon, I hauled the boat to California and found a woman near Oakland who agreed to loan me space at her dock in exchange for sailing lessons.

The trip with Gail had taught me that I was a good-enough sailor on a lake, but I needed to improve my ocean skills. I joined the Cal Sailing Club, where, for a nominal fee and some volunteer service hours, I had access to a fleet of fourteen-foot Lido daysailers and twenty-one-foot Pearson Ensigns. These larger keel sailboats had a large cockpit and a fixed lead keel running along their bottom. Unlike the Lidos, the Ensigns wouldn't capsize in the heavy winds that made sailing scary on San Francisco Bay.

To take out an Ensign, I first had to pass a sailing test on the Lido, showing that I could sail without a rudder, using only sail trim and center board adjustment to steer. I eventually got the hang of it and was qualified to sail the Ensign, but for some reason, I never did.

I spent Christmas with Mimi and her family, and in the spring Mother and Dad visited me. Karen Henry had moved to San Francisco, and she joined us as I showed my parents around. We took them to the Berkeley Marina and the San Francisco waterfront overlooking Alcatraz, and we viewed the city lights from the Berkeley hills. That summer, I rode my motorcycle back to Utah for a visit. Mimi and her family were there, and we stayed up late debating socialism and individualism.

Back in Berkeley, I moved into a shared house closer to the marina and tried to manage on my meager savings. I looked around for a teaching position, but the baby boom had swept through, and there were no jobs to be found. I was doing some substitute teaching in the South Bay area when I got an offer to teach sociology to parole officers in Oakland. The part-time job was through the Chapman College East Bay Extension. The school didn't have high standards; I had to prepare a syllabus, but in reality, no one at the school knew what I taught or how. I didn't do a very good job of it. I was also broke. I sent a message home and Dad sent me $25.

Chapman offered me another teaching job, this time teaching Navy seamen on a ship leaving out of San Diego, the USS *Bradley*. With Vietnam winding down (finally!), they were hoping to retain crewmen by offering free college credit courses, and I was assigned to teach two concurrent three-week sociology classes. In San Diego, I got a room at the Army-Navy YMCA and went shopping for second-hand paperback books; my plan was to have the servicemen read them and write book reports. I also had textbooks for my two classes, Intro to Sociology and Social Problems. I was eager to expand the perspective of the students.

It didn't turn out as expected. For a starter, my "classroom" was the enlisted men's lounge near the stern, just over the propellers. The racket was so loud it was hard to hear each other. Both classes were small, with

USS Bradley DE 1046, on which Ed taught during a three-week voyage to Subic Bay in the Philippines. On the foredeck is a five-inch gun, behind which is the housing for anti-submarine missiles.

a dozen or fifteen students in each, but because the men were all on different shifts, they couldn't make it to class consistently. I had expected them to have plenty of free time to study, but in reality they had hardly any. I later learned that the Navy's motto is, "Keep them (the crew) busy." The box of secondhand books was permanently stashed under a desk in the ship clerk's office; I doubt that the textbooks got much use, either. I spent my days with the enlisted men, ate with the commissioned officers, and bunked with the non-commissioned officers. I was living in three different worlds, all of them foreign to me.

The classes came to an end three weeks later, when we reached Subic Bay in the Philippines. I spent a few free days traveling around Luzon Island, experiencing, for the first time, a developing country from the vantage point of a privileged American tourist (my other trips to poor countries had been as a hungry student). What sticks with me today is the image of the Filipino girls shivering under the cold blast of American-style air conditioning in the giant hangar used as a dancehall at Clark Air Base. They'd been hired by the US military to serve as dance partners, waitresses, and bartenders for off-duty servicemen.

I thought about talking to the sailors about the ethics of taking advantage of third-world women, but in the end, I kept my opinions to myself. For servicemen, this was how the world worked: R&R in the Philippines meant getting drunk and getting a girl. It was a culture I wasn't going to change. A couple of days later, I flew home at the government's expense.

I moved again, this time into a house on Fifth Street. I had to share it with roommates, but it was closer to the marina. I tacked a notice to the bulletin board at a boat supply store saying I was available to crew a boat, and in September, Ben and Kathryn Porter from South San Francisco contacted me. Nearing retirement age, they had quit their jobs, sold their house, and used their life savings to buy a boat. Neither were experienced sailors, but they were planning a trip down the coast of California to Mexico with Ben as the captain. They were counting on whatever sailing expertise I had (it wasn't much). In preparation, I read *Two Years Before the Mast*, an 1840 memoir about the author's journey on a merchant ship along the California coast. I hoped to absorb some of the details about the weather and harbors of California.

Over the next couple of months, I made several trips to Oyster Point Marina in South San Francisco to work alongside the Porters on *Sansu*, a beautiful thirty-eight-foot wooden ketch. My parents loaned me a couple hundred dollars for my share of the food and incidentals, and in mid-January, after a practice run to Half Moon Bay, we set sail. From San Francisco we charted a course south, passing sea lions, seals, porpoises, and gray whales, the latter on their way to Scammon's Lagoon in Baja California.

Kathryn and Ben Porter working on their 38-foot wooden ketch, Sansu, in the fall of 1973

Sansu under sail along the California coast

Sansu plows into a wave along the California coast.

Because of the prevailing northwest wind, harbor-hopping toward Baja is like riding a bike downhill (coming back up is a different story). To save the fee for tying up at a marina, we anchored in harbors at night. Ben, nervous about his sailing skills, kept the diesel motor running continuously as a backup, and the noise and fumes got to be nerve-wracking. Occasionally rowing to shore in the dinghy was a relief.

We didn't have any storms, but we encountered some strong winds. Each time a gust came from behind, the boat would dip and slide sideways with the waves. Two or three times we didn't make it to the next harbor before dark and had to sail through the night. That was scary.

In less than a month, my trip with them came to an abrupt end. It happened when we were about halfway down the coast of Baja California, sailing at night. The navigation lights in Mexico aren't reliable, and we knew we had an island coming up along our path. I tried to convince Ben to head farther offshore, but he didn't want to get too far out. He won the argument but lost my confidence, and when we reached Turtle Bay, I jumped ship. We had an agreement that either party could back out if things didn't work out, but I still felt bad about leaving them in the lurch. It worked out for them, though, because they soon found a hippie couple willing to take my place as crew.

Turtle Bay wasn't much more than a village with a fish canning plant. It was too remote for buses, so I joined another traveler hitching on the side of the road. A sleazy-looking guy stopped and offered us a lift, but we turned him down. I didn't want to be one of the people you hear about whose murdered bodies turned up in the desert. We caught a ride on a grocery truck and got dropped off at the main highway, about twenty miles away. From there, I caught a bus to San Diego.

What I didn't know while I was making my way back to California was that my dad was lying in the hospital in Utah. He'd caught a bug while volunteering at the local VA hospital filled with returning Vietnam veterans. The bug turned into pneumonia, and Dad was admitted to the hospital. While there, he had a stroke. And then another.

Luckily, my family thought to look for me at the Army-Navy YMCA in San Diego, the same address where I had stayed before my stint on the Navy ship. I made it to Salt Lake in time to see my dad conscious. On March 31, 1974, two months before his 70th birthday, he died.

I had always been close to my family and my dad in particular. At his memorial service at the Unitarian church, I planned to stand up and say a few words about him, but the minister, Ron Clark, refused to let me. Apparently he'd experienced too many family members breaking down while giving a eulogy. It was a disappointment I have never gotten over. Decades later, that disappointment became the impetus for writing a book about Dad's life based on letters and his many journals. Working on *A Wider Horizon: The Primavera Journals of Ray Sabin* inspired me to write this book about my own life.

Betty in 1968; portrait by Ed (Betty didn't like her wrinkles showing.)

Ray in 1968; portrait by Ed

CHAPTER TWENTY-TWO

Joining the Establishment

In California, I was footloose, looking for a purpose and stumbling from one thing to another. I had opposed the arms race and the Vietnam War, but other than these issues, I hadn't much interest in national politics. However, when the international food crisis became a big story in the early 1970s, it captured my attention.

Even though American involvement in Vietnam was winding down in 1973, there were still other issues to worry about. At home, the fuel crisis was in full swing, and abroad, famine and civil war were killing millions. Editorials ran in the newspaper arguing the "lifeboat theory:" If we take too many people into the lifeboat, everyone sinks. The thought is that if well-fed countries share their wealth and food with starving nations, everyone suffers.

Of course many people, including me, disagree with this theory. One of my best classes at Michigan was demography, where we learned about causes of the tremendous growth in world population. Historically, the number of children born to a family decreases as a country becomes more developed and its population moves to cities to work where children become a liability instead of an asset. Because the death rate falls more rapidly than the birth rate, this is a period of great population growth. The US and Europe experienced this in the 19th and 20th centuries. I believe it's the responsibility of the industrialized countries to help developing countries through their period of high population growth, not throw them from the lifeboat.

I became deeply interested in the issue. In California, I gathered petitions to Congress sponsored by the American Freedom from Hunger Foundation, but I wanted to do more. With my education, I felt I had something to contribute. American food and development assistance policy is determined in Washington, DC, so I decided to go there and see what I could do. Now that we were almost out of the Vietnam War, Washington didn't seem like such a corrupt place. I sold the trimaran, and with a loan from my mother, I bought a little Vega and left for DC.

Gail had written to tell me she'd gotten a scholarship to Georgetown Law School, but it took only one night sleeping on her apartment floor in DC to realize our relationship was dead. I moved into a shared house in southwest DC, and with cheap rent, food stamps, and later, unemployment checks from my time substitute teaching in California, I was able to scrape by until I could land a paying job. In the meantime, I was getting a good education on how things worked on Capitol Hill.

At that time, churches were awakening to the fact that they needed to do more than just provide charity; they needed to get involved in politics and make their voices heard. IMPACT, a lobby organization of Protestant churches, put out a newsletter on public policy concerns such as hunger. I volunteered to help them produce it.

Their lobbyist, a Baptist minister, was savvy. He knew how to reach out to people and get them involved, and through him I learned the specifics of growing a mailing list, doing outreach, and soliciting contributions. I moved into a small apartment near Capitol Hill that was reasonably priced (probably because of the many cockroaches) and spent time attending legislative floor debates and committee meetings. Washington was a different world, both interesting and exciting.

My goal was to get on staff with the American Freedom from Hunger Foundation. They were located on M Street, not far from the White House, and Gerry Connolly (today a US Congressman representing a Virginia district) was the director. He resisted my offers to volunteer, probably because he guessed my real goal was to land a paying job. Finally, I convinced him that as a nonprofit, he needed a way to communicate with people and that it was crazy not to have a newsletter. He agreed and brought me on board as a volunteer to start one.

Our message at the Foundation was the opposite of the "lifeboat theory." We believed that it wasn't food that was lacking, but rather the political will to grow and distribute it. With the newsletter, we had the opportunity to inform and encourage people to take action to end hunger. IMPACT had been a good place for me to learn, because they had staff and seemed to know what they were doing, but Gerry's organization was a small, struggling outfit with a paid staff of only three: Gerry, his secretary, and an office manager. With so few of us, there was room for me to make a difference. The first editions of the newsletter were crude, nothing more than xeroxed sheets stapled together, but it was a start.

Our board chairman, Herbert Waters, had previously been a staffer for Hubert Humphrey. He had seen how Humphrey supported the US food aid program that sent shipments of wheat and soybeans to countries in need. He understood the importance of what we were trying to do, and he had some influence in DC circles. Occasionally we partnered with other organizations, such as the larger, more robust Bread for the World.

Our organization had gained some recognition when it sponsored a series of publicity events for World Hunger Day in 1973, and in 1975 we were awarded a USAID grant to continue our public education efforts. With the grant money, Gerry could now afford to put me on payroll, but he refused. By this time I'd been an unpaid volunteer for about six months. It wasn't until he saw me packing up my things to quit that he offered me a full-time position. I gratefully accepted.

Another new hire was Tim Sullivan, formerly of the Population Reference Bureau, a well-funded organization that produced publications much slicker than ours. With Tim's input, I learned how to create a more professional looking newsletter. Using an electric typewriter, I typed up four pages with two columns each, added some photos, and used plastic letter stencils to create headlines. Armed with a pair of scissors and a can of rubber cement, I did the paste up on a layout board, lining things up straight on the board's blue lines. The layout was then professionally photographed and turned into plates for offset printing.

Our main area of concern was health and nutrition in third-world countries, with a focus on mothers and children. In the developed world, the birthrate had tapered off, and some big corporations, hoping to grow sales, were running advertising campaigns for baby formula in poorer

Freedom from Hunger Foundation newsletter on breastfeeding. This issue was noticed by Naomi Baumslag, M.D., who offered Ed his next job assisting her as a writer/researcher.

countries. They covered billboards with advertisements, implying that formula was modern, healthy, and superior to breast milk. Not only were they trying to sell something poor people didn't need, they were doing it in places that didn't have access to clean water. Due to the expense of formula, families were diluting it with contaminated water, and babies were dying as a result. The marketing campaigns got international attention and caused an outcry. We decided to do an issue on breastfeeding, with the motto, "Breast is Best."

"Discussions for Singles" was the name of a social group run by the Rockville Unitarian Church in one of Washington's suburbs. For a few bucks to cover the cost of refreshments, you could drop in for a Friday evening discussion group, followed by dancing to a record player. I enjoyed these low-key events.

I also attended Sunday service at the All Souls Unitarian Church in downtown DC, and it was here that I met Carol. Originally from Kansas City, she was married to a Syrian mathematician who'd gotten himself into some kind of legal trouble and had been forced to leave the country. Carol and I started to date, and after a while, she asked me what my future career plans were. Maybe I wanted to go into business? She hinted that her family, a wealthy clan in Kansas City, might set me up with something. I told her no, I wasn't considering business. "I'm working for a cause," I said.

"I volunteered for Oxfam during college," she replied.

The implication was clear: Causes were for college kids, not adults. The relationship ended, but not without me trying to see her a few more times. She sent her brother to tell me to stop contacting her, which I did. Later I found out she had gotten pregnant. I hoped the baby wasn't mine, but it's something I can't know for sure.

Before he was promoted to director of the Freedom from Hunger Foundation, Gerry had recognized that the then director wasn't doing a good job and fought to have him removed. In a similar way, a few years later, I tried to have Gerry removed. Today he's a successful, articulate politician, but in the 1970s he was going through a rough period, and his frequent absences were hurting the foundation. In 1978, Matthew, another staffer, and I brought it up to the chairman of the board, and when Gerry learned of it, he got angry. My next move was a mistake. I sent a letter to another member of the board, someone I didn't know well, and we all ended up in a meeting in the chairman's office.

I didn't hold back. I told them about Gerry's behavior and how it was hampering the organization. Matthew, though, sensed that the board was in sympathy with Gerry and refused to back me up. In the end, the board believed Gerry's promise that he would shape up and do better. They fired me.

None of our names were on the newsletter, so the board members had no idea who was putting it together. Gerry had never been involved in the newsletter process, but he assured the board that he would put out the next issue after I was let go. Then, behind closed doors, he asked me to do it for him. I turned him down. A few months later—still with no newsletter—the board fired Gerry, too.

Out of a job, I took out my Rolodex and contacted everyone in it. Naomi Baumslag was a public health physician from South Africa with lots of field experience but little knowledge of Capitol Hill. She had received a contract from the Office of Nutrition at USAID to work on child nutrition and needed to staff her office in the Department of Health, Education, and Welfare building in Rockville, Maryland. She'd seen my issue of the newsletter about breastfeeding and offered me a job. She also hired Chris Roesel, a nutritionist and returned Peace Corps volunteer. He and I became friends.

I commuted from Arlington, Virginia, and spent time attending hearings on Capitol Hill; I'm a pretty good note-taker when I have to be. A special Congressional committee had been formed to study the Third-World infant formula issue, and I put together a six- or eight-page summary reporting on their hearings. Naomi sent it to everyone she knew. A couple of returned Peace Corps volunteers at the Office of International Health assumed that all this information was a matter of public record and implied that I had wasted my time attending hearings and taking notes. They didn't realize that the Congressional Record, which they assumed would have this information, covers only proceedings on the floor of Congress, not what happens in the dozens of committees where the real work of Congress takes place. I gave myself a pat on the back for being able to set them straight.

I was able to create content, do layout, and get reports printed fast. But to use the official HEW/Office of International Health designation, we were supposed to first submit the report for approval, a process that could take months. I got around it by attaching stick-on letters to the cover and an "official" HEW logo. We got called on it a few times, but it was worth it. Reports need to be timely if they're going to do any good.

I didn't miss the trimaran, but I did miss working on a boat. I fixed up an old sailboat that had been sitting out in a field for years and sailed it, but I wanted something larger, and a boat that would be sturdier than the trimaran. In 1976, I saw an ad in the *Washington Post* for a ferro-cement sailboat hull. A Georgetown law student had built it but had run out of steam and had abandoned the project. He had hired a low-boy truck to haul the hull to Calvert Marina in Solomons Island, Maryland, and I drove there to inspect it. At

The ferro-cement hull soon after Ed bought it in 1976. The boat was later named Aldebaran after a navigation star. Note the sheets of plywood on the roof of Ed's Vega.

some point, it had been dropped; a long patched-up gash ran along the bottom of the keel. By coincidence, a large ferro-cement Arab dhow—a type of sailing vessel—was under construction in the same boatyard. I asked one of the guys building the dhow to take a look at the sailboat hull. By his estimate, since the hollow keel would be filled with iron ballast and concrete, the patch wouldn't cause a problem. He said I could make it into a "funky crab-crusher"—-a boat that goes up and down with the tide, crushing any crabs unfortunate enough to be under it. I bought the hull from the student for $1,100.

As I'd done with the trimaran, I spent most of my holidays and nearly all of my weekends working on the boat. The Washington Metro was being built at this time, and dumpsters at building sites around the city were loaded with discarded building materials. Before driving down to Solomons, I regularly stopped to scrounge for pieces of plywood, two-by-six planks, and heavy pieces of rebar steel to use as ballast. I altered the original plans to give the boat a flush deck more in keeping with my crude carpentry skills and omitted an engine in order to save money. After two years, *Aldebaran* was ready to launch.

CHAPTER TWENTY-THREE

Love and Marriage

'd had serious relationships, but not knowing what I wanted in my life had kept me from making a lasting commitment to a woman. Sometime in my mid-thirties, I began to feel differently. I gave up on the idea that I was on a journey and was going to do something special. Instead I wanted to settle down, have a family and a normal life. Chris Roesel, my colleague at the Office of International Health, offered to introduce me to a friend, an ex-nun named Robbie Evans who taught high school in suburban Baltimore. "My office mate wants to meet women," he told her on the phone. "I guess I qualify," she said.

For our first date, I invited Robbie and her friend Anne to join me, Chris, and another friend on *Aldebaran*. Robbie and I hit it off (as a bonus, we also got to see each other in bathing suits). On our second date, we went for a bike ride at a reservoir north of Baltimore. I had plenty of experience dating, but that didn't mean I could pick up cues. I was too dumb to realize she wanted me to take her out to dinner after the bike ride; luckily, she wasn't shy about setting me straight.

Aldebaran under sail on Chesapeake Bay. Thanks to a push from Robbie, the boat's crude amenities had now been updated with a more comfortable cabin and an engine.

We began to see each other regularly, with me driving to northern Baltimore from Gaithersburg where I was living, or Robbie coming to me. Things were getting serious, and she introduced me to her parents, Bob and Delores, but unfortunately, I soon made a bad impression on them. The four of us signed up for a one-day bus excursion to Atlantic City, and as part of the package, we each received fifteen dollars' worth of quarters for gambling. At the end of the day, Bob and Dolores still had all of their quarters, but I had lost mine—plus an extra five dollars—at a blackjack table. They got the impression that I was some kind of riverboat gambler.

I was happy to have met Robbie. She was attractive, understood commitment, and appreciated a simple life, which, with my job history, was exactly what I had to offer. After three months, I bought an engagement ring. Unfortunately, the proposal turned into something of a non-proposal, thanks to my bumbling. We were at an outdoor café with some friends when I casually handed her a box in which I had packed the ring in a series of ever smaller boxes. By the time she got down to the last box and found the ring, people were watching and laughing. I assumed she understood that I was asking her to marry me, even without me actually stating the question out loud. When she didn't answer the question I hadn't asked, I took it as a sign that she needed time to think about it.

I didn't want to press her. Over the next few months, we didn't talk about it. Finally, on a walk in the Catoctin Hills, she brought up the subject, and I proposed on the spot. On March 29, 1980, less than a year after meeting, we married. We settled in Laurel, Maryland, halfway between her teaching job in northern Baltimore and my job (soon to end), in Rockville, Maryland.

Roberta (Robbie) Evans on a hike before marriage to Ed in 1980

Dr. Baumslag's contract with USAID ended about the time we married, so I was unemployed for a time. My next position was as a writer/researcher under another USAID contract with the American Public Health Association; once again, the focus was on health and nutrition in the Third World. I'm especially proud of a field guide a colleague, Mike Favin, and I wrote about delivering immunizations in developing countries. It was later reprinted several times by UNICEF.

About this time Ronald Reagan became president, and foreign aid spending, including the USAID budget, was cut way back. Once more, I had to decide what I wanted to be when I grew up. I took a French language class in DC thinking that would make me more marketable in the foreign aid business. A fellow French student, a government retiree,

Robbie and Ed married at St. Charles Catholic Church in Pikesville, Maryland on March 29, 1980.

Robbie meets Mother Teresa in Calcutta during a trip to India in 1981. Ed and Robbie traveled with other staff of the American Public Health Association to attend a conference there.

suggested I take computer classes, as this was an up-and-coming field. I immediately dropped the French class and began taking computer classes at our local community college. Several classes later I asked a teacher to edit my resume, and he took "technical writer" from the bottom of the page and put it at the top, renaming it "documentation specialist." I didn't know what that was, but I soon got a response from a contractor asking for an interview. That led to a position as a technical writer for RMS Associates, a NASA contractor located in the Washington suburbs.

Several years later, RMS undertook cost-cutting measures, and I lost my job. I talked it over with Robbie, and we agreed I should try part-time teaching as a strategy to get back into full-time college teaching, even though part-time teaching doesn't pay much. I taught part-time at Goucher College and Towson State University (TSU), among other colleges. Based on my computer experience, TSU brought me on as a visiting full-time faculty member. They planned to start a new PC computer lab, and a colleague and I applied for and won a National Science Foundation grant to build the lab. However, I made some mistakes which led me, after seven years, to not be asked to continue as a faculty member. One of these mistakes was when a colleague, Marion Cockey, asked to visit one of my classes. I didn't realize that this was not simple curiosity but part of the standard evaluation process for instructors. Instead of inviting her to visit my Intro to Sociology class, which I had down cold, I had her come to my research methods class, where I was trying to show students how to use a statistical software package on the PCs. Instead of teaching, I was running from one student's machine to another, trying to troubleshoot problems while other students were waving their arms waiting for help. It was chaos, and I'm sure the evaluation she wrote up reflected that.

So by 1995 I was looking for work (again). I'm indebted to Robbie for her patience with me bouncing from job to job at this stage in our life together. Her career in teaching, by contrast, followed a much smoother trajectory. After returning to school to earn a master's and then a PhD in computer science, she became a faculty member in the Computer Science Department at Loyola College. Her steady paycheck meant we had an income even during my periods of unemployment.

After losing the TSU position, I saw a help-wanted ad posted by the child welfare department for a contract statistician. I got the job, and a year later I became supervisor of the small research unit in the same department. This became my best job yet. In contrast to the half-hearted research I had previously done as a college teacher, I had the skills needed to do this job well. Also, I knew to not make a mistake my predecessor had made; that is, to fake data to make the agency look good. "That way lies madness," as my father would have said. I got a reputation for not sugar-coating unpleasant facts about agency operations. I had that job until I retired from state service in 2014.

John and Laura in 1988

When Robbie and I married, I knew we wanted children. I saw the joy that my parents experienced with their children and grandchildren as they grew older. Robbie, being from a small family, had not had that experience. After trying for a few years for home-grown children, we gave up and adopted two children from Korea. Laura came to us when she was four months old. She clearly had been well loved before we adopted her; she was an easy baby and everyone in the family fell in love with her, especially Robbie's parents. My mother lived in Virginia and we didn't see her often, but Robbie's parents lived nearby. Robbie took time off from teaching and after a time we found reliable day care.

When Laura was nearly two, I became fearful that all the attention that came with being an only child would turn her into a little princess, so Robbie and I decided to adopt again. At 45, I was deemed too old to adopt an infant, but Holt Family Services, the agency in Korea we worked with, agreed to let us adopt an older boy, Jun Hae Woong. John, as we named him, came to us in 1987 at almost five years old. Like Laura, he'd been well loved and cared for before the adoption, but our first years with him were difficult. We learned that in the Korean culture, male children are raised with little discipline in order to avoid "breaking their spirit." What happens when an irresistible force meets an immovable object? That was the case when two hard-headed people, John and Robbie, battled it out. I stood mostly on the sidelines wringing my hands. Eventually we learned to pick our battles.

Both kids have turned into wonderful, healthy adults with families of their own. As I write this in 2021, Laura and her husband Tristan Milstrey have two children, Josephine and Isaac, and live in a suburb of Phoenix, Arizona. John and his wife, Heidi (née Bowman), have one son, Kai, and live in Evergreen, Colorado (the same town where I spent my summers as a youth).

In 2017, we said good-bye to *Aldebaran*. Fortunately, she went to a guy who, like me, is a nut about boats and could appreciate her unusual qualities. Today, both Robbie and I are fully engaged in volunteer activities, including the Alternatives to Violence Project (AVP) in a state prison (me); a monthly book group at the women's prison (Robbie); the Ignatian Volunteer Corps and Marriage Encounter (both of us). We each have several other volunteer commitments as well. And we have

Robbie and Ed with Laura and John on a 2007 trip to Korea sponsored by Holt Family Services. Also on the trip were other adult adoptees and their parents. The purpose was to familiarize the young people with their birth country. A moving aspect of the trip was a visit to an unwed mothers' institution where Laura, among other youth, gave tearful testimony about being raised by parents who truly loved her.

traveled, both within the US and abroad. I accompanied Robbie on two Fulbright assignments to Africa, one in Malawi in 2013-2014 and another in Uganda in 2019.

Today I'm eighty-three years old and hope to live long enough to see how the crazy things going on in the world will turn out. Unlike Robbie, I don't believe in life after death; it's a one-shot deal. That's all the more reason to live fully and do what we can while we're here. Robbie claims she'll have the last laugh and that I won't get away from her that easily.